STOCK MARKET STRATEGY

STOCK MARKET STRATEGY

Richard A. Crowell

McGraw-Hill Book Company

New York   St. Louis   San Francisco   Auckland   Bogotá
Düsseldorf   Johannesburg   London   Madrid   Mexico
Montreal   New Delhi   Panama   Paris   São Paulo   Singapore
Sydney   Tokyo   Toronto

Library of Congress Cataloging in Publication Data

Crowell, Richard A
    Stock market strategy.

    1. Stocks. 2. Investments. I. Title.
HG6041.C76   332.6'322   76-43956
ISBN 0-07-014720-5

1234567890   KPKP   786543210987

The editors for this book were W. Hodson Mogan and
Carolyn Nagy, the designer was Elliot Epstein, and the
production supervisor was Teresa F. Leaden. It was set in
Melior by University Graphics, Inc.

Printed and bound by The Kingsport Press

CONTENTS

PREFACE

This book is a game plan for stock market investors. It describes how to make important decisions by putting them into an orderly framework. Without this, many investors waste time on peripheral matters and neglect the decisions of real consequence.

The book is written for every investor. It assumes only a basic knowledge of financial and investment terminology. Anyone who reads *The Wall Street Journal* or the business section of the Sunday newspaper will have no difficulty understanding it. The practical applications of several advanced concepts—the random walk, betas, capital asset theory, market analysis—are presented in clear, straightforward language.

Typical readers will have been in the market already, making decisions on their own or being aided by a broker or investment advisor. They will be searching for ways to improve their investment decisions. In game plan jargon, they already know the difference between a punt and a touchdown, and want to understand more about the strategy that goes into calling the next play.

Stock Market Strategy outlines three critical investment decisions: (1) setting your investment objectives, (2) evaluating the investment outlook, and (3) selecting stocks consistent with both the outlook and your objectives. The book provides understandable guidelines for making each decision.

INVESTMENT OBJECTIVES

Setting your investment objectives is the first and most important stock market decision. In the simplest terms, you should ask yourself: "What portion of my assets should be invested in the stock market?" The answer depends in part upon your financial situation. Investors who rely on their investments for current living expenses obviously have to be more conservative than high-income professional people who can afford to invest aggressively for long-term capital appreciation.

Psychological effects must also be considered. Those who suffer from investment insomnia—sleeplessness due to fear of the safety of their investments—should invest accordingly. A more adventurous strategy should be adopted only by those who can take the longer view, living with interim market fluctuations in hopes of eventual gain.

Chapter Four, "Risk and Diversification," provides clear-cut guidelines to assist in establishing your investment objectives. The chapter also shows how to determine whether your current portfolio is consistent with these objectives.

INVESTMENT OUTLOOK

Evaluating the investment outlook is the second key decision. History demonstrates that there are times for buying stocks and times when stocks should be sold. The stock market tends to vacillate between periods of greed and euphoria and periods of fear and despair; stock prices move up and down accordingly. There are clear signposts to suggest to the astute observer when to buy and when to sell. The irony is that investors often ignore the danger signals, allowing themselves to be stampeded by the mood of the times. Chapter Five describes the conditions that usually accompany important stock market peaks and troughs and provides checklists to help determine when such turning points are imminent.

STOCK SELECTION

Selecting individual stocks is the third step. Too often investors buy a stock on a whim or on the recommendation of a stranger when they should buy stocks that are consistent with their investment objectives. This book tells how to determine whether a stock is right for you. Does it have the proper risk characteristics for your portfolio?

It also describes how to select stocks that are appropriate in light of the investment outlook. Three important stock selection parameters— value, growth, and staying in tune with the market—are discussed and the functions of each of these at various phases of the stock market cycle are explained.

The search for value is a traditional investment approach. In Chapter Six, the basic principles are reviewed and standards are suggested to determine whether a stock is undervalued, fairly valued, or overvalued. All else being equal, undervalued stocks are favored, but one must be aware that undervaluation can go unrecognized and unrewarded for long periods of time.

Growth is another important parameter. Growth stocks have been the mainstays of leading institutional portfolios for years and are bound to be important in the future. Chapter Seven describes the reason why growth stocks attract so much attention. The chapter also outlines some of the pitfalls of growth stock philosophy as well as providing guidelines for timing growth stock investments and determining whether a particular stock qualifies as a growth stock.

The third approach to stock selection, staying in tune, offers the greatest opportunities and the most risk. The stock market has a tendency toward a particular theme at each point in time—a fad that attracts buying interest. Stocks consistent with the theme advance, often dramatically. The out-of-favor stocks may offer better value and superior long run growth potential, but they languish.

In Chapter Eight, clues are offered to help detect the current theme and to determine when it is ending. The market always has a theme which is supported by seemingly irrefutable logic, and astute investors will take advantage of it. Nevertheless, all themes come to an end, and investors must be able to anticipate the demise of the current theme and the ascendence of a new one.

STRATEGY

Notice that stock selection is the third and final step in the market game plan. Most investment books concentrate on stock selection, since most investors consider this the key decision. Stock selection can only be successful, however, in the context of your investment objectives and the investment outlook. A seemingly great stock can be totally wrong for your objectives. The stock may also be inconsistent with your investment outlook; even the best stocks take very severe beatings in adverse market conditions. To be successful, investors need a strategy that focuses on the key decisions—setting objectives, determining the outlook, and then selecting stocks—and provides guidelines for making each decision.

ACKNOWLEDGMENTS

In preparing this book, I have benefited from the accumulated wisdom and experience of many individuals. My colleagues in research at The Boston Company—David L. Beckedorff, David M. Booher, Francis R. DeAngelis, Richard C. Katz, Edward A. Nargizian, Richard I. Morris, Jr., and our leader for many years, Godfrey G. Howard—plus many others contributed important ideas and suggestions. The senior management of the company has been very farsighted in support of research and the creation of an environment conducive to progress. Mrs. Deborah Benedetti has been indispensable in preparing the last two drafts. I am especially grateful to my wife and family for their patience, understanding, and encouragement.

Richard A. Crowell

STOCK MARKET STRATEGY

ONE

The 80:20 Law

Over the past decade, more than 80 percent of the professionally managed portfolios in this country have performed worse than the stock market averages. Eighty percent! Four out of five of the allegedly best-managed pools of capital—whether mutual funds, pension funds, endowment funds, or trust accounts—are worse off than had they simply bought the stocks which make up the Dow Jones Industrial Average. In short, 80 percent of the brokerage advice, economic analysis, portfolio management and investment committees not only have been worthless but have lost money.

Dismal as it is, this record is not unusual. The 80:20 law permeates our society. Next time you see your neighborhood hardware store manager, ask what is selling best. You will find that about 20 percent of the hardware items account for 80 percent of sales. The other 80 percent of the items in inventory which represent only 20 percent of sales can be considered failures as products.

Advertising knows the 80:20 law. Of every 100 advertising dollars, 80 are wasted, and only 20 really attract attention to the product. The problem, of course, is that it is difficult, if not impossible, to tell in advance which 20 are going to be successful. Advertisers end up spending $100 just to get $20 working for them.

Similarly, most people can recall only an hour or two each day when they really accomplished what they set out to do. The rest of the day was spent in routine but unproductive activity. We have no idea how to eliminate the 80 percent waste. None of us is able to function at peak efficiency all of the time.

So too with investing. When compared to the 80 percent failure rate so common in modern life, it is not surprising that so much investment effort yields so little results. The record clearly shows that the major amount of effort is expended in an exercise foreordained to failure. In spite of their efforts, most investors cannot even keep pace with the market averages.

The question for investors, professional and amateur alike, is how to get into the 20 percent column, how to achieve success. To do so requires understanding why so many have failed in the past. Simply put, investors and professional managers fail because they concentrate their energies on investment decisions that are unimportant. Worse, their own prejudices and vested interests interfere with making correct investment decisions. In short, they too often let irrelevant matters influence decisions and, thereby, doom their investments to failure.

To illustrate, consider the following scene, which occurs countless times every day all over the country. It is the summer of 1973. Three professional investment experts are meeting in a lavish office overlooking the harbor of a major Eastern city. One, a portfolio manager, is responsible for the management of a multimillion-dollar pension fund. The retirement security of several thousand employees of a distant company is dependent upon his skills. Under his management, the assets of the pension fund have been spread around, diversified if you will, into 74 stocks, the largest holding being IBM and the smallest a disaster he doesn't mention even to his wife. The performance of the pension fund has not been good; it has underperformed the stock market for several years and, far worse, has underperformed other pension funds for three consecutive quarters. If this dismal performance continues, the portfolio manager won't have the fund and its management fee much longer.

A security analyst employed by the same investment firm also is present. His specialty is auto stocks, along with several other industries. He is supposed to keep the portfolio manager up to date on developments in the auto industry and recommend changes in the pension fund's auto stock holdings as appropriate. About a year ago, he talked the portfolio manager into buying General Motors for reasons that seemed awfully good at the time. Regrettably, GM has underperformed the stock market and the portfolio manager is, at present, not too happy with the analyst and his recommendation.

The third person at the meeting represents a large Wall Street brokerage firm. A very bright and personable young woman with connections throughout the auto industry, she knows everything that's going on or, on those rare days that she doesn't, knows exactly whom to phone to find out. Parenthetically, we should note that the broker's career is based on executing stock trades, not investment performance. Of course, over the long run, her success, her ability to convince her clients to make trades, is based on the credibility and accuracy of her investment recommendations.

The broker has come to this meeting to recommend switching the GM into Ford. She says Ford is more aggressively managed, more flexible as the number two auto company, less constrained by the Antitrust Division of the Justice Department. More importantly, she believes Ford has done a better job of positioning itself to take advantage of the shift to small cars. Mustang II will be a hot seller, and GM has yet to develop a viable competitive car. She feels Ford will outperform GM in the stock market and is out to get the orders to sell GM and buy Ford.

The in-house security analyst, however, is opposed to the trade. He originally recommended GM and still feels it will come through. GM is the strongest auto company, best able to deal with foreign competition. The skill and depth of GM's management is well known. If anyone can respond to the Mustang II challenge, GM can. Besides, GM is undervalued at present. As soon as some of the value is recognized, the stock will start to move and the original recommendation will work out just as he has been forecasting for months.

After an hour or so of friendly discussion, the meeting breaks up. The portfolio manager must now make the decision. Shall he switch to Ford or ride with General Motors? He spends another 2 days making up his mind, reading reports and telephoning other respected Wall Street experts in the field. Finally, he chooses Ford.

History will eventually prove that all that acquired wisdom and painstaking deliberation were wasted. While the three experts considered many factors, they couldn't foresee that the immediate future held a Yom Kippur War, an Arab oil embargo, rampaging worldwide inflation, and the worst U.S. recession since the 1930s, all of which resulted in a decline of nearly 50 percent in both Ford and GM. For the pension fund, and those whose retirement security was dependent upon it, the GM versus Ford decision was irrelevant. The investment experts concentrated on a tree, and ignored the coming forest fire.

Though irrelevant to the pensioners, this decision was of consequence to the three involved. To the broker, it meant a large order and a fat commission. To the security analyst who originally recommended GM, it meant his status and reputation in his own firm. And to the portfolio manager, it was a decision one way or another he would have to explain to the pension fund's trustees. Nevertheless, for bottom-line investment performance, this decision, typical of thousands made every day, was unproductive. It only contributed to the 80 percent failure rate.

What should the three experts have done that would have increased, not drained, the pension fund? How could they have better spent their time so they would have ended up with the 20 percent who are successful in the stock market? They should have concentrated their energies on three things. First, they should have determined the exposure to risk appropriate for the pension fund. It doesn't really matter that the fund is underperforming other pension funds. That kind of enormous pressure simply forces the fund to become more exposed to stock market volatility than it reasonably should. Perhaps the pensioners would be better off if only a portion of the assets of the fund were, over the long run, invested in the stock market and the balance placed in more conservative investments. As immutable as the 80:20 law is the fact that the stock market is a volatile place to put money. The pension fund should have been in the stock market only to the extent it could really afford being exposed to this risk.

Second, the fund managers should have been more concerned with the current market outlook. Where is the stock market likely to go over the next year or so? Are conditions favorable for a continued stock market advance, or does the evidence suggest a defensive approach? When the stock market collapsed and GM, Ford, and most other stocks dropped 50 percent, half of a lot of people's retirement security evaporated. No one remembers whether GM went down a couple of percentage points more or less than Ford. Both were affected severely. The portfolio manager was so eager to beat the market in the quarterly performance race that he never considered getting out altogether. He should have sold the GM and bought Treasury bills, an alternative that never entered his mind.

Our experts, like most investors, spent far too much time on the third and least important investment decision—what security to own. This is not to suggest that security selection is unimportant. Far from it. However, good security selection can be made only after the first two areas—risk exposure and market outlook—are determined. The discussion should have considered whether either of these two stocks were appropriate for the pension fund's risk tolerance. Then there should have been discussion of how these stocks were likely to perform in the current market environment. Is this the kind of stock that can hold up well in the late stages of a bull market? If not, why own it at all? Only then should the merits of the respective companies have been considered.

Yet according to conventional investment wisdom, security selection is the most important step. One might well ask why the conventional wisdom concentrates on security selection when the resulting long-term investment performance has been so poor. Why do investors insist on devoting the majority of their time to an activity that has brought them so little success? There are several reasons. We have already mentioned the personal biases of professional investors—to get the trading order, to save face on a previous recommendation, to beat the competition, and to keep the clients happy. Also at fault is the basic structure of the investment process with its improper performance incentives. If the sole purpose of investing is to beat the competition, one tries to do it even if it is the totally wrong objective.

The fault lies also with an improper reading of history, of incorrectly learning the lessons that the stock market has been teaching. Most investment experts have attained their expertise through the apprentice system. They learned through on-the-job training. Their wisdom is heavily dependent on their own personal experiences. The portfolio manager was worried about switching GM to Ford because he had seen many instances where one of two similar stocks did much better than the other. In our case, both went down the same amount. In other situations, one declined and the other rallied. If, and it is a big if, you could just get in the right one, performance would be measurably improved.

Also involved is the fact that vision improves with hindsight. After stock A has gone up and stock B has gone down, it is clear to everyone why it happened. Pick up *The Wall Street Journal* and read about all the good things happening to A's business and all the problems B is having. However, 6 months ago when we were deciding between A and B, it was very difficult to select one over the other. They both had good things going for them, and frankly, both had a few problem areas. A's problems disappeared and B's got out of hand. That is clear now, but no one could tell at the time. Now when you look at A, it's obvious why it's a winner. But not six months ago.

Try to apply the same approach today. Compare stock X with stock Y.

X has excellent business prospects. On the other hand, Y's future growth is clouded. But the price is low and the current dividend yield is generous. Which stock offers the greater potential return? Weigh all the evidence, get the best advice, and then pick a stock. Chances are you will be correct slightly less than half the time, no matter which way you choose.

This is true especially if you are absolutely convinced that X is superior to Y (or vice versa). If anything, certainty decreases the chances of success. Because if something is certain, it is already in the price. The market's basic function is to discount the future. Be sure that the market has discounted certainty.

The problem in stock picking is that the market is already ahead of us. Everyone else is trying to pick the best stock. The competition is fierce, so fierce it is almost impossible to succeed. In this matter, hindsight is a disadvantage because we forget how hard the last choice was. When faced with a new decision, we relate it to the old "obvious" choice and try to pick another stock. On average, 80 percent of investors fail at stock picking.

Investors' experience with overall market-timing decisions has also taught the wrong lessons. Short memory is again the problem. Exhibit 1-1 shows the severe down markets that have occurred in the twentieth century. When our three experts met in early 1973, there had been only three meaningful market declines since World War II—1962, 1966, and 1970. For the current generation of investment managers, severe bear markets were a Depression relic long since forgotten. Once in a while we get a minor setback of 30 percent or so. Big deal. The long-term trend of stocks is up, at the rate of 9 percent a year, according to the experts at the University of Chicago. There is no point, they say, in missing the long-term uptrend just to avoid occasional interruptions.

Along came the 1973–74 bear market decline of nearly 50 percent. Investor sentiment changed. Now everyone is an expert on market timing. Everyone is aware that bear markets tend to come along every 4 years just as they did early in the twentieth century. The long-term uptrend of stocks is virtually forgotten as investors fearfully await the next bear market—so they can sell all those stocks they neglected to sell in 1973. In reality, this is only another example of investors' remarkable tendency to learn the most recent lesson, to prepare for the last war.

The conventional wisdom that dominates current investment decision making has led to widespread disappointment and disenchant-

EXHIBIT 1-1

Twentieth Century Bear Markets

(Declines of 25% or greater)

Dates	Duration, Months	Percent Decline
Sept. 1899–Sept. 1900	13	−32
June 1901–Nov. 1903	29	−44
Jan. 1906–Nov. 1907	22	−48
Nov. 1909–Sept. 1911	22	−27
Nov. 1916–Dec. 1917	13	−40
Nov. 1919–Aug. 1921	22	−47
Sept. 1929–July 1932	34	−89
Sept. 1932–Feb. 1933	6	−38
March 1937–March 1938	13	−49
Nov. 1938–April 1942	42	−41
Nov. 1961–June 1962	7	−29
Jan. 1966–Oct. 1966	9	−26
Dec. 1968–May 1970	18	−36
Jan. 1973–Dec. 1974	23	−47
MEDIANS	18–22	−41

ment with equity investing. With a fail rate of 80 percent, that wisdom must itself be classified as a failure. The basic methods must be rethought and new approaches considered, learning from the mistakes of others. We do not need a revolution—for, as we shall see, some of the conventional wisdom has merit—but we do need to refocus on the elements of the investment world, rearranging them along lines that are theoretically correct and practical as well.

Instead of the hustle and bustle of stock picking, investors need to focus on three major steps in investment decision making. We have already discussed the three elements:

1. Establishing how much risk you can take. How much can you afford to be exposed to the absolute volatility of the stock market?

2. Forecasting the investment environment. There are many clues to this seemingly impossible task, which involves discipline, investigation, judgment, and insight. But it is vital! As we shall see, the fortunes of the overall stock market determine, by and large, our own success or failure in the market.

3. Security selection. Stock picking is relatively easy once the first two hurdles are passed. The rationale for investing in a diversified list of strong, dominant, growing companies will be presented. If the market is heading up, investment success is assured by being in the strong companies. It is axiomatic that the rich stocks will get richer and equally true that if the market is heading down, no stock is safe.

So far, 80 percent of conventional investment wisdom and 80 percent of current investment practice have led only to failure. Many investors have good reason to be disillusioned with stock investing. Yet we are at a crossroads in the investment world. Their bitter experiences—and the intermittent successes—combined with recent advanced research provide a unique opportunity for both the professional and individual investor. The long-term trend of the stock market will be up, as it always has been. Sufficient knowledge, moderate self-discipline, and an understanding of the three principal elements of the stock market will guarantee an investor joining that small minority that succeeds.

TWO

Students of the Market: An Oversupply

We've explored why 80 percent of all investors do worse than simply investing in a broad market index. How does one become a successful investor? Is there any way to join the 20 percent who consistently do well? What approaches to the stock market are best?

There are no simple answers, but there *are* answers. To begin, it is helpful to review the advice of investment experts. Generations of investors have played the stock market. Even though most have been failures, they have learned from their bitter experience. They do have something to say, and of course, some of the successful investors have profound insights. Our first step then is to review the best advice that the experts have to offer.

It quickly becomes apparent from a study of stock market experts that there are many of them. Stock market success can be so rewarding financially, as well as psychologically, that many are attracted to the game. This is particularly true during strong bull markets when well-publicized gains attract many new "experts," most not worthy of the name. But that's always been true of any risk-taking venture. Every boom, whether it be a gold rush or oil gushers, attracts experts as well as the uninitiated looking for an easy buck, and, of course, promoters looking for the uninitiated.

But why, one should ask, are there so many widely divergent views by experts on how to succeed in the market? The primary reason is that the stock market is such a poor teacher. Like no other game, it keeps changing the rules for success. There are no constants, no relationships that can be depended upon to apply every time, no easy rules of thumb to guarantee investment success.

As a result, different observers see different patterns, different rules for success much like the varied reactions to a Rorschach blot. One individual's experiences in the market lead him to one conclusion, while another's lead to an entirely different one. Yet it's the same market and same opportunities for both.

If we looked at the stock market from the point of view of radio and communications engineering, we might say that the market has a very low signal-to-noise ratio. That is, there is a lot of static, hissing, and buzzing interfering with what's really being broadcast. If we listen long enough, we begin to think the hissing is part of the music, that some of the extraneous noise is meaningful, if not the purpose of the broadcast. We thus would tend to perceive a pattern in a patternless situation.

In college psychology courses, there is a basic experiment on super-stition in which a caged pigeon gets a peanut every time it pushes a certain lever. The pigeon learns which is the key lever only by trial and error, so it pecks away around the cage and eventually pecks the lever and receives the peanut. As time passes, we observe that the pigeon has learned that the lever has something to do with winning the peanut. But it turns out that this is not all it has learned: the pigeon soon associates its little ritual—a dance of jumps and turns and multiple pecks—with getting the peanut. From its point of view, the rain dance is just as important as the lever. It wouldn't get the reward without it. A further experiment has the peanut come out at random intervals without the lever being pecked. Nevertheless, the pigeon still does its ritual dance even though absolutely none of its activity influences the arrival of the reward. It sees a pattern where there is none.

It's commonplace for humans to see patterns where there are none or where they are distorted by randomness and noise. Perception of the real signal requires diligence and objectivity, something that's too often absent, especially when it involves money. There are many stock market experts. Some of their knowledge is worthwhile, but much of it is unconsciously distorted and misleading. A successful investor has to glean the 20 percent of available knowledge that is really valuable.

STOCK MARKET PROFESSIONALS

Stock market wisdom permeates American society—in the press, aca-deme, and, of course, politics. How often have we heard a U.S. President saying, "If I had any money, I'd be buying stocks now," and subsequently seen the market tumble to a new low. We begin our analysis with the professionals because they are the ones who have been most intimately involved with the stock market, who have played the game for all of their careers, through good times and bad. What have they learned in a lifetime of confronting the market? What bits of wisdom can they shed on our situation today?

Dismissed immediately are those who claim to have a gimmick or a system for beating the market. Those treatises entitled *How I Made a Fortune through . . . and You Can Too* are virtually useless. Wall Street is a place with no secrets, where every day hot new systems are born and die of old age before lunch. If there is a way to make an easy million or two in the stock market, it's already too late by the time most of us hear about it. The secret to making a killing in the market is just not available in paperback for $1.95 plus tax.

How did that expert make a million (other than from writing a "how-to" book for gullible readers)? Most likely what he did was take a lot of risk and get lucky. In fact, the risk was so great he had an excellent chance of losing all of his investment and possibly a whole lot more. Essentially, he played long odds and hit, as do the big winners at the race track or Las Vegas. Good for him. But don't try the same thing unless you fully appreciate the risks and the consequences of losing.

Of course, those "make a million" books can be of minimal value in giving a better understanding of such investment vehicles as options or commodities or whatever the game might be. And it's certainly true that from time to time, when conditions are right, an aggressive investor might want to allocate a portion of his assets to that sort of thing. But remember that the spectacularly big winner made his million by taking an enormous risk and being enormously lucky. Somewhere there are a lot of people who did the same thing, but lost. Losers don't write books.

THE GENERALISTS

A large body of stock market experience has been recorded by professionals who can be labeled generalists. They are generalists because they do not have any single formula for success, no system guaranteed to succeed no matter what happens. Rather, their writings are filled with general guidelines for making investment decisions based on their years of actually making such decisions, some right and some wrong, and years of watching others do the same.

Gerald Loeb was one of these. His books on the stock market almost always have the word "battle" somewhere in their titles, which correctly tells you that you are going to benefit from the experience of an old, scarred veteran. Loeb's works are compilations of essays on various subjects, different stock market problems and decisions that come up from time to time. For example, in a section entitled "Losses" in *The Battle for Stock Market Profits,*[1] he starts with, "I am a great believer in cutting losses short and attempting to keep unrealized profits from turning into losses." This general statement leaves a lot of latitude. He doesn't tell us how far the stock might fall before he'd cut his losses or even what might influence him to sell sooner rather than later. He says if the situation isn't strong enough to warrant an additional purchase, maybe you ought to sell. When in doubt, liquidate.

The cynics will suggest that this imprecision shows the futility of the entire approach. But for someone holding a stock that is off 50 percent and wondering what to do, the somewhat vague advice of the generalists may be just what is needed. They have been through it all before. And under certain circumstances, their suggestions can so fit your current situation, be so relevant to your current dilemma that it can seem almost like divine guidance. They have experienced your situation many times, and knowing how they got through, even if they muddled it a bit, can be very helpful.

It would be impossible to attempt to summarize Loeb's advice or that of any other generalists. There is just too much there that has to be read and reread as circumstances change. Loeb does offer us his own "non-formula" for investing, but only as a way of increasing the chances of stock market success. First, know yourself. If you are unsure, invest half in government bonds and half in leading investment trusts. Second, if you are learning about the market, proceed gradually. Make small, infrequent trades and keep substantive amounts in cash. Then, when you're ready to invest seriously, Loeb suggests the following guidelines: Take losses quickly. Don't overdiversify. Keep a cash reserve. Most people overinvest. "More losses are caused by overinvestment than any other single factor I know outside of downright ignorance and cupidity," says Loeb.[2]

Very general advice. No specifics, no formulas guaranteed to bring

[1]Gerald Loeb, *The Battle for Stock Market Profits*, Simon & Schuster, New York, 1971, p. 139.

[2]Ibid., p.347.

investment success. Just the wisdom of someone who has been through it all many times. We should pay more attention.

GROWTH STOCKS

The most philosophical professionals are those who espouse the virtues of growth stocks. This group is after the new IBM, the new Xerox, the next McDonald's. They want to get in early. Then, as earnings compound over the years and growth carries the company to new successes, the stock price will reach ever greater heights. Growth-stock advocates point to the wealth of early investors in IBM as proof of their claim that large fortunes are rarely made through stock trading. But, they argue, many have been created by concentrating in one successful company and holding on through the years.

The growth-stock approach has considerable merit. The only problem is how to find and recognize a new Xerox early on, when it is still small and not yet detected by the majority of investors. How do you tell the next Kodak from among a thousand or so choices, most of which will never amount to anything? This is where growth-stock philosophy is important. Growth-stock advocates preach that you must have well-conceived standards for selecting growth stocks and then stick with your stocks as long as the stocks continue to meet the selection criteria. If they are growth stocks, don't sell them no matter what happens to the stock price or the stock market in the interim. Stand by your growth-stock philosophy, holding growth stocks as long as they are growth stocks and only selling when you lose confidence in the company as a growth stock.

What is a growth stock? What criteria should be used in selecting tomorrow's successes today? Different growth-stock advocates would give you different answers, but most would be variations on the same theme. One good example is presented by Philip A. Fisher, a prominent West Coast investment advisor, in *Common Stocks and Uncommon Profits*.[3] Fisher lists 15 distinct points to look for in growth stocks, almost as if he were reviewing thoroughbreds at a Kentucky auction. While we will not review all 15, a few of the major points are: whether the company has products and services to make substantial increases in sales in the future, a management determined to develop new products to replace the current ones when they reach maturity, a substantial

[3]Philip Fisher, *Common Stocks and Uncommon Profits*, Harper & Row, New York, 1960.

profit margin, good labor relations (growth companies don't ever have strikes), management depth, effective cost controls, standing relative to competitors (growth stocks are always much stronger). Additionally, one may ask whether equity financing which will dilute the profits of the current investors will be required, and whether the company has a reputation for integrity (growth stocks never have scandals).

In summary, a growth stock is a company with products and services certain to be successful, already clobbering its competitors, clobbering them fairly in the market place (nothing illegal, of course, just honest success), with high profit margins, financially solid, and of course, with top-notch management in all the best meaning of the definition— depth of personnel, integrity, and dedication to long-range planning and earnings growth.

This could be called the Boy Scout investment philosophy because companies with all these characteristics are destined to succeed. Unfortunately, such corporate qualities aren't identified by merit badges. The problem is to determine in advance if the profits are going to grow, if the products will be successful, and if the management is solid and honest before the first crisis hits. Given the vagaries of the business world and human nature, these things are, if not impossible, difficult to forecast.

Growth-stock advocates appreciate the difficulty of the task. They realize that any investment approach requires difficult decisions which must be made correctly. They argue that the long-term odds are on their side, that at least they are trying to make the correct decisions. Consequently, they claim the best chances of success and point to all those wealthy holders of Coca-Cola as proof.

It would be inappropriate to leave the growth-stock philosophy without reviewing a common ideology of most of its advocates: the futility of market timing, that is, anticipating market ups and downs and investing accordingly. There is no reason that growth stock advocates must necessarily be negative on market timing, but the vast majority are. Perhaps one reason is that growth-stock investing is a convenient way to avoid the market-timing problem. People just hold their growth stocks through market rallies and collapses, trusting in the long-term growth of the companies. Growth-stock advocates just seem to believe that picking growth stocks is less difficult and more profitable than timing the market.

In *Common Stocks and Uncommon Profits*, Fisher illustrates this view. In his chapter on "When to Buy" he suggests that having bought

25 good stocks at the market peak in 1929, just before the greatest market crash in this century, would over many years have been very profitable, though obviously not as successful as waiting a few months and buying the same stocks at lower prices. "If the right stocks are bought and held long enough they will always produce some profit," he says.[4]

Timing is secondary to Fisher. He sees little value in economic forecasting, finding the forecasters too often wrong and too often in disagreement with one another. As a result, Fisher suggests timing only to the extent of buying a growth stock when the rest of the financial community has temporarily lost faith in it, such as when new product promotion expenses are adversely affecting profits or the expenses of opening a new plant depress profits for a short period. This is a kind of stock-oriented market timing which does not relate to any overall market cycle.

In summary, "Unless it is one of those rare years when speculative buying is running riot in the stock market and major economic storm signals are virtually screaming their warnings (as happened in 1928 and 1929), I believe this class of investor (growth-stock investors) should ignore any guesses on the coming trend of general business or the stock market," he says.[5] Instead, you should invest when your growth stock is favorably situated, and that should be the extent of your interest in market timing.

As we shall see later, this is a grievous error. Even the best growth stocks—and Fisher is correct in insisting growth stocks are the best stocks—can experience severe losses in bad markets. Worse, they all tend to drop at the same time with a devastating effect on a portfolio of growth stocks. Thus, we would argue, it is essential to combine growth-stock investing with a sense of market timing. Market timing will be dealt with later in this chapter.

INTRINSIC VALUE

Benjamin Graham appeared frequently in the financial press, especially during bear markets. He was described as "a vigorous seventy-nine," living at his La Jolla condominium overlooking the Pacific or summering in southern France, busily translating ancient Greek or rewriting

[4]Ibid., p. 63.
[5]Ibid., p. 75.

the latest edition of one of his books on investment. Before retiring, Graham was a broker and fund manager for many years, one who was constantly on the firing line. His colleagues say he was always willing to do what was sound from an investment viewpoint rather than follow the popular Wall Street fad of the moment.

Graham is best known for coauthoring a massive tome entitled *Security Analysis.*[6] First published in 1934, the fourth edition contains 778 pages. Despite the length, the subject matter is tightly restricted to detailed, in-depth analysis of individual securities. The entire emphasis is on solidarity, objectivity, and discipline. The only thing that even mentions speculation is a 60-page section entitled "Senior Securities with Speculative Features." This chapter turns out to be a review of convertible bonds and convertible preferreds. On the risk spectrum, these are only slightly more aggressive than bonds, much more conservative than most common stocks. In short, hardly speculative at all.

The conservative, nonspeculative approach taken by Graham and his associates was to determine the intrinsic value of a security through a careful analysis of the underlying corporation. They went at length into techniques for analyzing the historical financial records of the company, its balance sheets, and income statements for the past several years, based on the assumption that the future of the company is an extension of its past.

There are several acceptable methods for determining the intrinsic value of a security. One is to determine the underlying value of the assets owned by the company. The factory building is worth so much, the machinery, properly depreciated, something additional, and so forth. Another approach is to determine the real earning power of the company and capitalize those earnings at a fair price/earnings (P/E) multiple. This requires tearing into the financial statements to ensure that past earnings were sound, with no accounting gimmicks to inflate (or understate) true earning power. Projections of future earnings are made with great caution, always within the context of earning power derived from analysis of the record. Then, a fair P/E is determined. What is fair? Something conservative that the stock has sold at many times in the past. No nonsense about a P/E the stock might achieve in the future. Rather, a low conservative number from the past experience of the stock.

---

[6]Benjamin Graham, David L. Dodd, and Sidney Cottle, *Security Analysis,* 4th ed., McGraw-Hill, New York, 1962. (Used with the permission of the McGraw-Hill Book Company.)

One thinks of real estate appraisers coming into your home with a tape measure. They count the number of baths, measure the floorspace, measure the size of your picture window, evaluate the neighborhood, and, of course, trot down to the City Clerk's office to see what your house and similar houses have sold for in the past. Then they seal themselves in their offices for a time while they do calculations, double-checking their arithmetic. Finally, they write a report telling you the appraised value of your house to the penny.

Ben Graham appeared more frequently in the financial press during bear markets, when stock prices were heading down and investors were hoping prices would stop declining when they reached their intrinsic values. One preferred not to hear from Graham during a bull market, not just because his whole approach was boring. The real problem was that he was such a barb to the conscience. Here we were making money in the market, having a grand time, and Ben Graham came along and said paying more for a stock than its intrinsic value was speculating, not sound investing.

Benjamin Graham realized the unpopularity of his approach. He was quoted frequently to the effect that *Security Analysis* was the most widely read and widely ignored investment book he knew. He wasn't inflexible either. Each succeeding edition had been revised somewhat to reflect the temper of the times. Who knows? Maybe someday stock market investing will return to intrinsic value and the solid approach advocated by Graham and his associates. After all, he has retired a wealthy man, which is more than a lot of present-day money managers can say.

The type of sound fundamental analysis of a company recommended by Ben Graham certainly has great merit. It can do much to help avoid investing in financially unsound companies, thus having considerable defensive merit. And, on occasion, one runs across a truly undervalued stock that can provide excellent returns.

There are two problems, however. First, undervalued securities often remain undervalued for long periods of time. If you are the only one recognizing the intrinsic value, you may wait a long time for your reward. The second problem is the overwhelming number of security analysts. There are so many prospectors in the gold fields that all the good claims are already registered. It is almost impossible to find a real bargain—simply because most have been discovered already. There are so many good analysts that they cancel out one another. Sound fundamental security analysis is important—but don't expect it to uncover many real bargains.

MARKET TIMING

Another large school of investment professionals advocates investing based on timing the overall stock market cycle. In their view, which is at odds with intrinsic valuers, the most important investment judgment is to distinguish bull markets from bear markets. If it's a bull market, almost every stock will rally, and making money is easy. In a bear market, almost every stock will decline. In short, the credo of the market timing advocate is "buy low, sell high," a truism joked about and occasionally ridiculed, but nevertheless followed by a large number of investors, directly or indirectly.

Graham's *Security Analysis* has a chapter critical of market analysis. The opening sentence summarizes his viewpoint. "Forecasting security prices is not properly a part of security analysis."[7] Period! Graham et al. then proceed to outline their views on the shortcomings of market timing, taking shots at chart reading and the like. They take particular pride in disputing one Colonel Ayres, who in a 1922 pamphlet suggested that stock prices usually reach a bottom when blast furnaces in operation decline through 60 percent of the total. Conversely, security prices usually top when blast furnaces in operation pass through the 60 percent mark on the upswing.

Despite the criticism from *Security Analysis*, the virtues of buying low and selling high are patently obvious. While the methods for deciding what is high and what is low may differ, we should all like to be able to do it. Even *Security Analysis* advocates this approach indirectly. Buying stocks below their intrinsic values and selling them when prices soar far above intrinsic values is simply a variation of buy low, sell high. If there are few stocks around that seem to be selling below their intrinsic values, perhaps the market as a whole is overvalued. Intrinsic value is just another form of market timing.

Colonel Ayres and his 1922 treatise on blast furnaces is another form. The stock market has a tendency to rally during expansions in the general economy and to drop during declines in the economy. The relationship is not precise, of course, and is further complicated by the fact that the market tends to lead the economy. For what it's worth, the stock market is officially classified as a leading indicator of the economy by the U.S. Department of Commerce and others who make this type of study.

[7]Ibid., p. 711.

Colonel Ayres was apparently reflecting this phenomenon in his study of blast furnaces and pig iron production. Iron and steel were an important component of the U.S. economy in the early days of this century. Ayres was no doubt observing that when blast furnace operation was off sharply, the economy was in a major recession and stock prices were no doubt down as well. Since recessions, even depressions, don't last forever, stock prices were probably in an attractive zone.

On the other hand, Ayres suggested selling when 60 percent or more of available blast furnaces were in operation. Market advances and economic expansions do not last forever. Long before the economic expansion has run its course, the stock market begins to see the coming economic peak and starts down. The market starts to drop while the economic expansion is still progressing. In Colonel Ayres's day, only 60 percent of the blast furnaces were in operation and the market peak was near.

Steel and Colonel Ayres's 60 percent rule probably were excellent bellwethers in their day, but like Colonel Ayres they were temporal. However, the underlying principle that there is a strong tie between the market and the economy remains sound and of great use today.

The monetary approach is a closely related component of market timing. An expansive Federal Reserve Board policy, especially in the face of a weak economy, is usually positive for the stock market. On the other hand, tight money almost invariably leads to declining stock prices. The reasons for this have to do with how monetary policy affects the economy and the fact that the market leads the economy—a fundamental truth too often ignored. Indeed, it is this close interrelationship that makes the monetary policy/fiscal policy argument so difficult to resolve. They are so closely intertwined that a conclusive statement on one alone is almost impossible.

THE TECHNICIANS

Still another component of market timing is a social measurement— considering the behavior of various investors under different market conditions. The market is people, not stocks. It therefore is dominated at times by greed and rampant speculation and at other times, by fear and panic selling. Many investment professionals pay close attention to these trends as clues to the future course of the market. They tend to look on rampant speculation (greed) as a sign that a bull market is about to end and a possibly long-term bear market to begin. These tend to be periods when stock prices sell far above intrinsic values and, ironically, when the economic outlook is particularly rosy. Investor optimism and an economic boom, combined, historically result in overpriced stocks; a market peak is not far from sight.

On the other hand, technicians consider investor fear and panic selling as a great buying opportunity. They reason that when everyone is panicking, usually because the economic outlook is poor, stock prices are most likely undervalued and it is time to buy. That is correct unless what is happening is a collapse of the economic system, as many will be saying at all points of a severe market decline. What is to many a selling climax, by which the decline hits bottom, is to others a momentary pause on the way farther down.

Investors who follow this sort of approach are called technicians, for they look at the so-called technical aspects of the market. In this context, technical refers to prices, price changes, and trading volume. The opposite is fundamental analysis, the Graham and Dodd approach of analyzing the company itself and such fundamental factors such as assets, sales, earnings per share, and other financial and accounting data. A pure technician is one who would look at a chart of stock price and trading volume and make a buy or sell decision without even knowing the *name* of the company.

The technicians believe that the stock market reflects the collective wisdom, ignorance, or human behavior of millions of investors. By watching the collective and easily documented decisions unfold, they hope to detect changes in investor expectations about a stock or the market before any underlying fundamental changes are widely known. Technicians would look for growing investor interest in a stock and, when they found it, might recommend purchase of the stock even though they, the technicians, had no idea what was motivating the investor interest. In a sense, technicians hope to anticipate the fundamental analyst, the one looking at individual companies. By watching price and volume changes, they hope to buy before fundamental changes become widely known.

Technicians see investors as a mindless wolf pack, near starvation, desperately foraging through the deep snow for their dinner. Technicians wait quietly, watching from a high vantage point, as the frenetic search for riches proceeds below them. Suddenly the wolf pack catches a scent on the wind and rushes off, howling, in a new direction. From their vantage point, the technicians see them change direction, spot the new prey, and sweep in for the kill before the pack arrives. While their profit motivations are the same, the technicians believe you can learn more by watching the antics of others than by trying to catch the scent yourself. Without the fundamentalist wolf pack to spy out the land, technicians would be hopelessly lost. But with their own quickness and intelligence, they hope to profit without getting their own feet damp in the deep snows.

Technical analysis applies both to the stock market as a whole and to individual stocks. Technicians usually have reams of charts on both the overall market and hundreds of stocks. They analyze hundreds of trading factors and make judgments without regard to the economy, earnings of companies, and so on, because they believe that the market knows before economic and fundamental analysts ever catch on.

There are a variety of technical approaches, probably as many different ones as there are technicians. And all technicians insist that experience and judgment must be applied along with the charts, for one cannot make decisions blindly on the numbers and patterns alone. Nevertheless, an example of methods used by one leading technician in evaluating the prospects for the stock market may be of interest.

Joseph Granville, considered by many the father of modern technical analysis, is the author of *A Strategy of Daily Stock Market Timing for Maximum Profit.*[8] The terms "daily" and "maximum" let us know immediately that Granville's is not an idle, passive approach, but going for the jugular every single day. Intensity pulsates from every page.

Granville offers no less than 55 basic day-to-day indicators to evaluate the daily outlook for the stock market. The first indicator says, "When the number of declines outnumbers advances together with a rise in the Dow Jones Industrial Average, then the market is on the verge of a decline." In short, if most stocks are down on a day when the popular averages are up, watch out. The stocks in the averages are diverging from the overall market trend, and this usually leads to disappointing performance in the averages.

Rule Number Two is the opposite of Number One. If the averages are down on a day when most stocks are up, watch for a rally in the averages. The other 53 indicators evaluate the averages, the breadth of the market, trends in trading volume, disparity between two different market averages—the railroad average usually leads the industrial average—and so forth.

It is unfair to say technicians look only at prices and volume and

---

[8]From the book, *A Strategy for Daily Stock Market Timing for Maximum Profit* by Joseph Granville © 1960 by Prentice-Hall, Inc. Published by Prentice-Hall, Inc., Englewood Cliffs, N.J.

never at economic conditions or company fundamentals. Few technicians would, in practice, be so narrow in their investment perspective.
Granville himself lists other conditions that necessarily must be considered in making judgments about stocks and the market. For example, his 1962 description of the conditions prevalent at major market
peaks sounds very much like what actually occurred at the market peak
in 1973—high industrial production, long delivery delays, shortages,
overexpansion of credit, overvaluation of stocks with many selling at 2
percent yields, rapid increases in commodity prices, low bond prices,
inflated real estate prices, high inventories financed by heavy bank
loans, and so forth. Those who could not remember the past bear
market were condemned to repeat it in 1973.

THE ACADEMICS

As we've shown, the only certainty in the stock market is the diversity
of approaches of knowledgeable, professional investors. Their
investment philosophies are a confused mixture of utilizing, or ignoring timing, of owning or disdaining growth stocks or ones with intrinsic value, of buying today's fads or yesterday's losers, of watching
companies or studying charts. Experience, one must conclude, teaches
a variety of lessons.

By contrast, almost without exception the academic authorities on
the stock market have a rigidly doctrinaire approach to investing that is
a curious offshoot of Ben Graham's intrinsic value school. The business
schools and economics departments academics who pontificate on the
stock market live by three tenets—value, the random walk theory, and
something called the capital asset pricing model. These are actually
extensions of one another, in effect forming a unified theory of investments based on the common premise that investors are rational profit
maximizers and have access to the same information.

The academic concept of value is that stock prices reflect investors'
consensus view of the present value of anticipated future earnings or
dividends from owning a stock. To them, a common stock itself is an
investor's right to a stream of future dividend payments much like a
bond representing rights to a stream of future interest payments. The
stock price is the investors' current assessment of the value of those
future dividend payments. Since the stream of dividend payments is
uncertain, changes in investors' estimates of the level and growth of
future dividends result, according to those in academe, in stock price
changes. Also, the discount rate that investors apply to these dividends

fluctuates with interest rates and the degree of uncertainty connected with the dividend payments. At any given time, however, the current price of each and every common stock reflects investors' consensus estimates of the present value of future dividends from the common stock.

At this point, the difference from Benjamin Graham becomes apparent. To academics, stock prices are already a fair reflection of value. There is little point in looking for undervalued stocks because almost all stocks are now fairly valued. That's the job the stock market is supposed to do—value stocks fairly. If it does, no stocks will be undervalued or overvalued. It is precisely because Graham's disciples do such a competent job of detecting undervalued securities and bidding them up to fair prices that academics believe stock prices are indeed fair reflections of value. There are no undiscovered bargains in the stock market because security analysts do such a good job of ferreting them out. Actually, this is one of the few points where some minor disagreements appear within the ranks of the academics. Hardliners will say that no undervalued situations can ever be found. The more liberal academics will allow that there might be a few now and then. But not very many, and then probably hardly worth the cost of finding them.

Following directly from this line of reasoning is the "random walk" theory, one of the most widely publicized market theories of recent years. It holds that if today's stock prices are fair representations of value, stock prices should not change in any systematic way. Stock prices will change only if something unexpected happens, like an oil embargo or economic downturn, for example. Since investors do not know whether the next news report will be good or bad, academics claim no one can predict whether the next price change will be up or down. Consequently, say the theorists, stock price changes should be random. The "scientific" term for such a phenomenon is a random walk, that is, movement without pattern, design, or purpose.

According to the random walk theory, a stock price has no memory; it doesn't recall that yesterday it went up, and what it did yesterday has no influence on what the price will do today. Yesterday's market rally doesn't mean that the stock will continue to rally or will decline today. Yesterday doesn't mean anything about today.

One implication of the random walk theory is that all systems for beating the market must fail, particularly the technical systems based on finding meaning in stock price movements. Since stock price changes are completely random, there is no meaning. Furthermore, according to the random walk theory, attempts to extrapolate price trends cannot succeed. Even sophisticated technical systems which attempt to find complex patterns in price behavior are only seeing mirages, according to advocates of the random walk.

Moving on from random walking, if stock prices are fair reflections of the value of a stock and if stock price changes are essentially random, how is it that some stocks provide higher returns than others? Or, more correctly, how can we construct a portfolio that will have a high expected rate of return? The answer is found in the third area of the academic viewpoint, the capital asset pricing model.

The capital asset pricing model says that high return is associated with high risk. If you want to earn a high rate of return, you must be willing to bear great risk. In this view, the capital markets pay high expected return to those investors willing to bear extra risk. By expected return is meant return on average over a long period of time. In any given period, the rate of return may be low or even negative, due to risk. If investors are willing to take a chance of a loss, even a substantial loss or a total wipeout, the market will on average pay them a high rate of return—if they can stay around long enough. But in the short term, the return may be very much more or very much less than expected.

According to this view, an owner of high-risk stocks should expect to receive a high rate of return in the long run. In any given period— today, this week, this year—that risk may work against the high-risk portfolio to the point that it may experience substantial losses. Consequently, a high-risk portfolio probably will increase in value rapidly in a good market and fall rapidly in a bad market. A more conservative portfolio probably will move in the same direction but to a lesser degree. In the long run, the high-risk portfolio should have the higher return. Not necessarily, of course, because risk means that nothing is certain.

The capital asset pricing model goes on to describe some ways of estimating the risk of particular assets and therefore, their expected returns. This subject will be dealt with in more detail later. The key point is that risk and return are associated. You cannot expect high return unless you are willing to bear risk. But risk does not guarantee return. It is only a necessary ingredient. You also need knowledge and skill, and luck.

In spite of a unified view of a rather elaborate theory of investments in general and the stock market in particular, the academics have made very little impact on the way investments are made. Every day, billions of dollars are invested with total disregard for the academic viewpoint. One reason that the academics and their plethora of learned journals and seminars are largely ignored by market professionals is the academics' very lack of practical experience. Since they have never had to decide what to buy or sell or had to explain an investment loss to an irate client, academics are considered inherently and eminently unqualified to comment on the real world. To investment managers, academics are grandstand spectators who would find it a different world down in the muck and mire of the playing field.

This problem is intensified by a massive communications gap. Most of the academic literature on investments is written in highly mathematical, esoteric jargon that even other academics—the main audience—don't always understand. Too, very few academics even seem interested in bridging the communications gap. If it is to be bridged, it is the responsibility of the academics to drop the academic jargon which requires so much specialized training to comprehend. But, unfortunately, many academics don't think fostering greater communications is worth the trouble because, in their view, investment professionals are hopelessly irredeemable in giving up their outmoded investment approach for a better one. This conflict will endure, most assuredly.

We also must keep in mind that there is resistance to the academic view because it really isn't much fun. It is a difficult, disciplined, tightly reasoned, and impersonal viewpoint based on objective, scientific analysis. In a word, dull. Investors want the thrill of victory, the agony of defeat, the exhilaration of the investment battle. We don't want to hear that the latest big winner is just good luck, not a reflection of our brilliance and skill at picking stocks. It's the seventh game of the World Series. It's the bottom of the ninth; the bases are loaded. The Dodgers and Yankees are tied. Koufax is on the mound. In the stands 60,000 are screaming and another 100 million are glued to TV sets as Mantle steps to the plate. Do we want to hear Mel Allen exclaim "going, going, gone"? Or, is it time for a diminutive, spectacled chap to step to the mike and state, "Statistically speaking, the probability of a hit is zero point three one five"? The academics take all the fun out of an exciting game.

THE MONEY GAME

"Adam Smith," our generation's Adam Smith, had a lot to say about people versus the academic viewpoint. His 1967 publication, *The*

Money Game,[9] is one of the most entertaining and informative books ever written about the stock market. It quickly topped the bestseller lists because it was more about people and human nature than about the stock market. *The Money Game* underscores the point that people are a lot more important than the market because people often invest for irrational, psychological reasons totally unrelated to making investment profits. The stock market is a giant game where the money gained or lost is the way to keep score. "Adam Smith" knows stock market profits aren't spent on yachts and sports cars. Those things are only mobile advertisements for who's winning and who's losing the game.

The Money Game, as the author describes his book, is a practical view about the image, reality, anxiety, and, by the way, money that make up the stock market. The pseudonymous Mr. "Smith" (in real life a Wall Street veteran before becoming a full-time author) underlines the view by quoting John Maynard Keynes. Not Keynes, the fabled economist, but John Maynard Keynes, speculator. While both were the same person, history little notes that Keynes the speculator made a fortune for himself and his college, Kings College, Cambridge—all in a half hour each morning from his bed. Unlike most academics, Keynes was perceptive on markets because he had that "feel" that can only come from participating—from playing the game.

The Money Game dismisses the academics for more than their grand-standers' lack of experience in the stock market. Academics are in error on their most basic assumption, he says. The academics assume that investors are rational, economic men who invest in the market to maximize their financial profits. This to "Smith" is nonsense. He can find no one in the market who is rational and whose purpose is to maximize his economic returns. Instead, he introduces us to the founder and head of a giant mutual fund complex controlling billions of dollars in the stock market who believes personal intuition more important than rational judgment. Imagine an individual who employs scores of sophisticated security analysts and portfolio managers, believing more in intuition than all that skill and knowledge.

If that isn't enough to destroy the rational economic man assumption, consider some of the other people "Adam Smith" meets in the stock market. There's Edward, who sold out his inheritance of Avon just before it went up tenfold, because it wasn't his *own* selection but came from someone else in his family. Or, Arthur, who made eight

[9]"Adam Smith," *The Money Game,* Random House, New York, 1967, pp. 55–68.

times his money in Solitron, and now feels terribly guilty because he didn't buy more. "Was I dumb!" he says. Or there's the gal who owns Comsat because it's so lovable.

None of these are rational, economic persons in the market to maximize their profits in a financial sense. The only way you could call it profit maximation would be to count the psychological value far more important than the money. You'd have to have a way of evaluating the well-being of someone who feels happier when he loses. The capital asset pricing model would have a lot of trouble with that.

The Money Game's biggest salvos, however, are aimed at the professionals. The author finds the professionals guilty of getting more satisfaction from building the system, whatever it is, and seeing it operate on a day-to-day basis, than they do from making profits in the stock market. The thrill of being in the game is far more important than the profits made or lost. The big-time money managers want to walk into Oscar's and have all heads turn and everyone ask their opinion on what to buy. The quest for fame and glory, and just plain fun of playing the money game, are a lot more important than the money. In *The Money Game*'s irrational, but very, very human stock market, all the techniques and systems for making money are about as important as a child's toys. And worth about as much.

SUMMING UP

The professionals and the academics possess so many conflicting views of how to convert lead into gold that investors are tempted to doubt any will work. The professionals disagree among themselves so violently, in fact, that we are led to question the value of experience. Then, the academics tell us the professionals are doing such a good job at running an efficient market that the whole thing is a random walk. Finally, "Adam Smith" insists no one really cares about the gold. The process of trying to make lead into gold is rewarding enough in itself.

Alchemy for modern man has a connotation of falseness and futility, even deceit. Considerable resources were wasted on a hopeless objective. However useless the practice, there were some profitable developments. The early alchemists floundering about attempting the impossible learned a great deal about chemical processes. In so doing, they developed the foundations of an important modern science.

These students of the market have developed important insights into the functioning of the stock market. They do not have the whole process of converting stock market lead into gold and likely never will. But they have developed a foundation of knowledge that can be helpful to those who seek to learn from them. Their contributions are basic steps on the path to a successful stock market strategy.

THREE

Bobby Fischer and the Random Walk

No concept so clearly distinguishes investment professionals from their critics, particularly the academic type, as the allegation that stock prices fluctuate randomly and no expertise is required for investment success. This concept undermines the very foundations of security analysis and portfolio management as currently practiced by thousands of investors. If stock price changes are random and unpredictable, there is no point to knowledgeable analysis of the stocks most likely to advance and to aggressive management of the securities in your portfolio. If the investor can't anticipate the winners from the losers, he might as well stick with the portfolio he's got. When he has some spare cash, he just picks a few stocks at random, buys them, and forgets them. There's nothing else for him to do.

Professional investment managers know from experience that this is nonsense. Dangerous nonsense at that. Stock prices don't fluctuate randomly; there is a reason for every price change. The stock market rallies on good economic news—growth in gross national product, declining unemployment, stabilizing balance of payments—as well as favorable political and international events. It declines just as quickly on news of wars, recessions, and economic setbacks. In addition, individual stock prices react to the company's changing business fortunes—good or bad earnings, a new contract, a favorable merger, a new product or an acquisition.

Clearly, events, not random movement, cause stock price changes. These events need to be tracked and studied, and every effort made to predict them. Indeed, responsible professional investors have to, or else how can they expect to understand the stock market and correctly make the decisions that are required to attain sound investment performance?

But the debate continues. Academics continue to publish learned studies applying advanced statistical techniques, all pointing to the random character of stock market prices, that stock prices follow a so-called "random walk." Investment professionals generally ignore this criticism of their craft, plunging ahead with investment decisions based on traditional analytical tools. Neither side is able to convince the other or change the way the other operates. Further, a communications breakdown exists, almost as though each side has its own untranslatable language it doesn't care to have others understand.

There are three primary reasons for this communications gap. First, few investors understand what the random-walk argument really says about stock prices. Rather, they often assume random means meaningless, without cause, which it does not. Second, few understand the positive applications of the random walk to practical investment management. Attention is too often focused on the negative implications: because of the random walk, you can't do certain things. But random walk advocates do indeed have some positive advice to investors that needs to be applied. Third, insufficient attention has been devoted to what it takes to beat the random walk. Despite allegations to the contrary, it is indeed possible to beat a random walk. There are many examples, both from the stock market and from other situations, showing that outstanding individuals have consistently succeeded where the random walk concept says they should not. Bobby Fischer's consistent success against the Russian grandmasters is just as difficult as earning superior returns in the stock market, if not more so.

WHAT IS A RANDOM WALK?

The basic principle of the random walk is that there is no free lunch. You can't get something for nothing. The stock market is not a charity providing handouts to the needy. It is a tough battle among many worthy adversaries who provide strong competition to any and all participants. In this contest, you don't win anything you don't earn. Competition assures that there are no quick and easy profits to sharpies trying to outsmart the market. The other participants in the market are just as sharp and aggressive and they are not about to let someone else run off with an extra profit if they themselves see it first.

As a result, stock market transactions take place at competitive prices, prices that *both* the buyer and the seller deem reasonable. The buyer buys because he thinks the stock is undervalued or, at worst, fairly priced. He never buys because he thinks a stock is overpriced. On the other hand, the seller sells because he thinks the stock is overpriced or at worst fairly priced. He never sells because he thinks the stock is too cheap. A seller sells what he considers a richly priced stock to a buyer who thinks he's getting a bargain. And, on average, they are both equally correct. Their competition results in a standoff, with the vast majority of stock market transactions taking place at what the broad consensus of millions of stock market investors consider fair prices.

One must be quite careful here when discussing bargains and over-valuation. It is incorrect to equate stock market prices with some objective standard of intrinsic value. Rather, the decisions are based on the individual's estimates of future rates of return from holding the particular stock. Someone may indeed sell a stock he considers cheap, based on his own subjective standard of value for that stock. But he sells anyway because he feels the stock will not provide above-average rates of return in the fairly immediate future. He feels the true value of the stock will remain unrecognized by the market. Similarly, a buyer may buy a stock he considers overvalued on the basis of some objective standard of value because he believes it will become even more over-valued, thus providing him with a superior rate of return.

The competition between millions of buyers and sellers, all investors trying to make a favorable return on their investments, means that stock prices fairly reflect the future returns from holding particular stocks. There is no way to tell which stocks will provide superior returns that has not already been thought of by other investors. There is no way to predict which will go up and which will go down on a particular day or month or year. One stock has just as good a chance as any other.

But stock prices do change. Some are up and some are down every day. Since competition in the marketplace implies these changes can-not be anticipated by investors, these changes must be essentially random. It is as if someone were flipping a coin to decide whether a stock will be up or down today. And tomorrow the coin is flipped again, and so on the next day. As a result, stock prices wander around, up and down, irregularly and unpredictably, in a manner that statisti-cians call a random walk.

EMPIRICAL RESULTS

The real test is whether stock prices *do* behave randomly, not whether stock market philosophers think they should. This subject has been studied in great depth, using a variety of statistical approaches. Three examples of empirical testing of the random walk may be of interest— the bell-shaped appearance of stock price changes, the performance of randomly selected portfolios (dart throwing), and overall mutual fund performance.[1]

The first test has to do with the appearance of stock price changes. Consider the price changes of the 500 common stocks in the Standard & Poor's Composite market index during 1972. (Exhibit 3-1). While there are a few big winners and a few big losers, the majority are clustered around the middle in the traditional bell-shaped or normal distribution

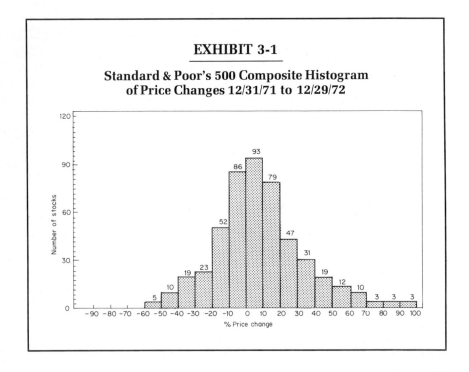

EXHIBIT 3-1

Standard & Poor's 500 Composite Histogram of Price Changes 12/31/71 to 12/29/72

[1]For brevity, these arguments are vastly oversimplified. For a more complete analysis, see Paul Cootner, ed., *The Random Character of Stock Market Prices,* MIT Press, Cambridge, Mass., 1964.

so common in statistical analysis. This suggests that the underlying process is itself random.

The second test concerns well-publicized stunts in which various public figures (U.S. senators, typically) throw darts at a musty, old newspaper's stock market page. About 20 or 25 stocks are selected in this manner and combined into a hypothetical portfolio. And, to no one's surprise, the "portfolio" performs as well as the stock market averages—and beats a number of professionally managed mutual funds.

Finally, there is the record of mutual funds in total. One might think that this group of professionally managed funds would surely beat the market. After all, the pros have the best security research, the best portfolio managers, the best information sources. With all of this, one presumes, they should be able to beat the market.

But numerous studies show that, on average, they don't. While some mutual funds have outstanding records, mutual funds, on average, have slightly underperformed the stock market as a whole. The performance gap depends on the period selected, but it's often near one-half of 1 percent per year. That is, the average mutual fund has trailed the market by about one-half of 1 percent per year.

Some funds have outperformed this dismal record, but few persist in displaying superior performance over the long term. In fact, studies have shown that a fund outperforming the market in one year is no more likely to outperform in the next year than any other fund. An underachiever from the first year is just as likely to outperform in the second year as a fund that was successful in the first.

THE VALUE OF INFORMATION

To advocates of the random walk theory, these statistical results confirm conclusively that stock market success is largely a matter of luck, of just happening to be in the right place at the right time. Knowledge and skill have little to do with it, they say. Consequently, the advocates continually argue that the knowledge and skill of investment practitioners is of no value, that they can't even beat a dart thrower.

How can this random walk view be reconciled with that of experienced investors who know that events do influence stock prices? Very simple. Usually one does not know of the event until after it's reflected in the stock price. Suppose a company reports poor earnings. If the poor earnings were expected by investors, most likely the stock price has already declined. The price declined as investors first became aware of the poor earnings prospects and thus was discounted when the bad news actually was reported. On the other hand, if the poor earnings are a surprise, the stock price reacts to the announcement. The price drops immediately, before anyone—or practically anyone—can get a sell order to the broker.

To beat the market you must anticipate events that affect stock prices *before* other investors anticipate them. You must be the first to forecast that a company's earnings will be good or bad and be the first to see a recession or economic boom coming. And you must act on that forecast. You must do this in competition with other investors who are just as smart, work just as hard, and have the same or greater resources at their disposal.

There is one additional complexity—to beat the market, you must be the first to anticipate the future using the *same* information that is available to everyone else. Inside information—information on the prospects of a company that is not available to other investors—is forbidden. It's against the rules of the game. And the referee, the Securities and Exchange Commission, assesses severe penalties against violators.

These are the basic tenets of the random walk school: Buyers are as smart as sellers, and sellers are as smart as buyers. They all have access to the same information. So stock market transactions must take place at prices both consider fair, prices that properly reflect a security's prospects. As a consequence, stock prices cannot change in any simple, systematic manner which both parties can predict. Stock price changes must be essentially random, say the advocates.

What this really means is that there are no simple ways to beat the stock market. Stock prices already reflect the obvious, and stock prices do not change in any systematic way. Naive methods of selecting stocks—such as throwing darts at a newspaper's stock price page—are as likely to select a portfolio to beat the market as any other.

IMPLICATIONS FOR INVESTORS

As we shall see, the random walk theory has some serious deficiencies. But it also has its strong points. It adequately explains a great deal of every investor's stock market experience and has important practical lessons for all investors. For the moment, let's assume the random walk theory is accurate and explore its implications.

First, since you cannot get something for nothing, don't try. Don't pay attention to investment systems, no matter how sophisticated the system or its inventor. If the system requires nothing of you—other than a payment to its inventor—it probably will return nothing to you—other than costing you the price of the subscription. This criticism applies to all types of market systems—technical systems that evaluate stock trading data, graphs, computers, averaging systems, and whatever else the inventive mind develops. No matter what the system, no matter how convincing the historical record, don't ever think its going to give you something for nothing.

Even the most sophisticated investors get trapped by the system approach, hoping to get something for nothing. Consider the widespread interest in growth stocks in 1973. The system was very simple—buy growth stocks, hold onto them, and you will beat the market. Clearly, if this simple system were to succeed, it would be an outright violation of the random walk. Such an approach should not succeed, and the record shows that it did not.

Gold bugs have long advocated gold mining shares as the way to beat the market. But according to random walk advocates, gold stocks cannot be more attractive than anything else. And over a long period, they haven't been. True, gold stocks did well in 1973, but this barely makes up for many years of dull performance. This is not to criticize growth stocks or gold stocks or any other stocks as invalid investments. The only argument is they are no more attractive over the long term than other stocks because, to repeat, you just cannot get something for nothing in the stock market.

The other side of the "can't get something for nothing" coin is that you cannot lose something for nothing, either. Many investors who have suffered losses in the market blame some sinister force or conspiracy for their lack of success. The random walk argument rules this out. While you may have been unlucky and someone else more successful, there is no conspiracy involved. Your competitors in the market are struggling just as hard as you and, on average, with just as little or just as much success. In fact, the best proof that there is no evil conspiracy is the mediocre investment results of those most often accused of dominating the market. The records of the big institutions are underwhelming. Brokers alternate between feast and famine, depending on the success or failure of their clients. The overall record of brokerage investment recommendations is consistently mediocre—just ask their large clients. So don't think you were losing because someone was fleecing you.

A basic tenet of the random walk is that investment information flows relatively freely to all investors. Actually, the information doesn't have to go to all investors, just to enough to balance off the price at a fair level. This means that most investment information is reflected in the stock price before anyone can profit from it. So information that is generally available to other investors is not going to enable you to get ahead of the competition. It just enables you to keep up, to understand why prices are at the current level, not which way they are likely to change.

One implication of widespread information and the resulting fairness of stock prices, basic tenets of the random walk theory, is that you need not fear being underinformed. If you are interested in investing in a large, widely understood stock with the objective of achieving a fair—not above average, but fair—return on your investment, you need not fear buying because you are not the expert on that stock that someone else is. All the available information is already in the stock price so the price is probably a fair price. If someone knew that bad news was about to come out, the stock would probably already be down sufficiently to compensate for the bad news. The inverse applies to good news. So if you are buying for long-term prospects of a fair return, you need not fear being underinformed about that particular stock if it is widely held and widely studied by other investors. If you do happen to buy just before the price drops, be assured that you are just as surprised and chagrined as everyone else.

An absolute guarantee of success in the market, of course, is to have specialized (but not inside) information that is not widely known or widely understood by the other investors. This is extremely difficult to obtain, but from time to time all of us have this opportunity in limited ways. For example, if you happened to notice a few years ago that a new hamburger stand with high golden arches was very popular with the neighborhood children and seemed to be opening many new branches all over town and in other nearby cities, you might have been one of the lucky ones to stumble onto McDonald's.

Similarly, an enterprising person might have been one of the first to see a demonstration of the Xerox copying machines, foreseen its explosive growth, and bought the stock. Or a frequent traveler might have observed the popularity of rental cars and have been an early buyer of Hertz or Avis. This kind of specialized information is available to everyone and requires only intuition, astute interpretations, and risk taking. Any of us can come across similar opportunities and can do very well by utilizing this specialized information.

There is a fine line of distinction between specialized information and inside information. Inside information is illegal and usually applies to information obtained from company insiders—directors, officers, or high employees of a company. Special information is information available to anyone on an unrestricted basis which may not be widely appreciated or understood. Of course, superior analysis and investment judgment based on generally available information is clearly legitimate.

Finally, the random character of stock prices implies that diversification is critical. If you concentrate your investments in one stock or a handful of stocks, you run a grave risk that unexpected events will turn against you. You may read the paper some morning to see that your favorite stock has dropped 20 percent or more for some reason that no one could anticipate. If all your assets are in that stock, your wealth has diminished 20 percent. Diversification can cushion both the probability and the degree of loss, but it also reduces the opportunity for gain. Appropriate diversification, not putting all your eggs in one basket, is a key implication of the random walk.

CAN YOU BEAT THE RANDOM WALK?

The random walk argument is simply another way of describing open and fair competition. It is the application of the Adam Smith free market system to one special area—the stock market. It is an elaboration of the thesis that all are equal, that anyone has as good a chance of winning as everyone else. The stock market, a merciless equalizer, plays no favorites; big or small, rich or poor, institution or individual, all have the same opportunity to be right or be wrong.

The random walk argument applies to every competitive situation, not just the stock market. Any fair contest in which competitors with equal access to resources—including information—will have the same characteristics. None of the obvious ways to beat the pack will systematically win. Someone may happen to be in the right place at the right time and succeed. But that's luck—randomness again. Someone else will probably win the next round.

Many examples illustrate the application of the random walk to competitive situations outside the stock market. Take for example the National Football League, in which 28 professional teams compete through a 14-game regular season. The eight teams with the best records then enter a three-round elimination to vie in the Super Bowl game. The Super Bowl winner receives national publicity, acclaim as the world champions, and significant monetary rewards.

The fair-game aspect of professional football is best typified by the annual player draft. Players are the key resource, and fairness is built into the system by giving the teams with the worst records the first choices in the annual draft for new players, meaning also that those with the best records get to choose from among the least desirable players. Consequently, anyone who develops a successful team eventually will be faced with a serious shortage of new talent. Since football players wear out quickly (the average career is less than five years), staying on top for an extended period is extremely difficult.

The record bears this out. The Green Bay Packers dominated football and the first two Super Bowls in 1967 and 1968. Within a few years they fell to near the bottom of the standings, while once talent-poor teams like the Miami Dolphins and New York Jets subsequently rose to the top. Despite the sportswriters' proclamations each year of the beginnings of a new dynasty, the structure of the draft makes pro football a fair contest.

No team can hold a monopoly on talent. All of the upcoming college players are known quantities. Indeed, information flows so freely that many teams participate in scouting pools, sharing information on college players. Consequently, any team has just as good a chance as the others at drafting the best players. Rarely can one use extra resources (money, for example) to buy the best team. The competition is fair, and any team can move up.

WINNING CONSISTENTLY

Pro football, the stock market, and many other contests are fair games that anyone can win. By definition, where anyone can win the winner is not predetermined by some biased process. The crucial question is whether it is possible to be a consistent winner. Is it possible to consistently beat the market, to consistently win the Super Bowl? The previous arguments suggest that it is not because fairness implies anyone can win. There is no monopoly on success in a fair game.

Actually, this is a bit of a distortion, because fairness does *not* mean that anyone can win. It means that the best will win. Fairness ensures that there are no limitations on becoming the best, save one's own resourcefulness.

There are competitive situations analogous to the stock market where consistent winners have appeared. Chess is one. Chess is certainly a fair competition, matching individual against individual, where nothing is secret and nothing is left to chance. All the chess pieces are right there on the chessboard in full view. Both players can calculate the various possible combinations. All relevant information is fully available to the competitors, just as in the stock market.

The random walk argument should be applicable. Two opponents of the same quality should be approximately equally matched. So world championship chess matches should be very difficult to predict, with the outcomes essentially random. Indeed, this has been true in the postwar period. There have been frequent shifts in the holder of the world championship. And, many of the 24-game world championship matches have been so close—12½ to 11½, for example—that the winner could hardly be considered the more skillful.

For all of this, Bobby Fischer's performance in winning the chess world championship in 1972 was clearly not a random walk situation. The record demonstrates that Fischer was far more than the luckier of equally matched players. He won the 1970 interzonal tournament to determine challengers for the championship by scoring 16 wins, 7 draws, and 1 loss, winning the last 7 games in a row. He won the three challenger elimination matches 6–0, 6–0, and 6½–2½, and dethroned Champion Boris Spassky 12½–8½ after trailing 0–2 on a blunder and a forfeit.

The odds against such a performance were astronomical. Fischer clearly was far more than lucky. Obviously, he did not succeed through inside or special information. The arrangement of the pieces on the chessboard is apparent to everyone. Somehow he was able to evaluate the available information—and make superior decisions. And he was able to do this consistently against the very best competition.

There is an abundance of other examples from a variety of competitive situations, including business and investment management situations as well as sports. The point is that individuals or groups have been able to succeed consistently in fair competitive situations far beyond what could be expected from a strict application of the random walk. They succeeded because they were able to evaluate the information available to everyone else and consistently make better decisions. Their judgment, not their spy system, was superior.

In the stock market, on average, the buyers are as smart as the sellers. All have the same information. The key is to find ways of evaluating information that provides a decided, consistent edge over the competition and help to outperform the stock market averages over a period of time. The examples from chess and athletics do not tell us how to beat the stock market. But the contests are sufficiently similar—equally matched participants making decisions on readily available information, turning in consistently superior results—that we are encouraged to attempt the same thing. If Bobby Fischer can beat the Russian grand masters, if the Dolphins can win the Super Bowl, then even the lowliest of investors can beat the stock market.

FOUR

Risk and Diversification

On Monday, April 23, 1974, the common stock of Consolidated Edison, the giant utility providing electricity to the New York metropolitan area, closed at $18 per share. The next day, citing various financial problems leading to lower earnings, the Board of Directors of Consolidated Edison announced the company could not pay its quarterly dividend, the first dividend omission by ConEd in many decades. The common stock of Consolidated Edison dropped sharply on the New York Stock Exchange. There were so many sellers that the specialist had difficulty maintaining an orderly market. By the close of trading, the stock was at $12.25, off more than 30 percent from the last trade before the announcement. Overnight, investors in what many considered a safe, solid investment supplying a resource that New York City could not live without, had lost $300 million.

This was not an isolated instance in the spring of 1974. Combustion Engineering dropped from $76 to $51 in a single day on the basis of a broker's research report that alleged that the company had contracted to build several nuclear power stations at prices below cost. Polaroid, one of the darlings of the growth stock cult of a year earlier, dropped sharply when quarterly earnings below expectations were announced. Westinghouse Electric dipped suddenly on rumors that the company was short of cash and on the verge of bankruptcy. The fact that these rumors were false and the company's subsequent announcement that it had arranged a $500 million line of credit with major banks did nothing to help the stock price.

These events and countless others that could be recited show the magnitude of stock market losses that can be incurred in only a single day. Over a few weeks or a few months, even greater losses can occur. The common stock of General Motors, the largest industrial corporation in the world, dropped from over $80 to below $40 as a result of the energy crisis and the bear market of 1973–74. IBM, the largest company in the world in terms of the market value of its common stock, dropped from about $350 to nearly $150 in about 18 months, a loss of nearly $30 billion. For smaller, more volatile companies, the percentage losses in many cases were far greater.

This is risk: sharp, sudden dips in price or slow but steady erosions of value, which cause investors to wonder whether there is any downside limit short of absolute zero. Hard-earned assets are evaporating, and nothing can be done but hope they will one day recover.

Stock market investors must be aware of the risks inherent in all common stocks. The risks in *all* common stocks are substantial, no matter what their past record or current sponsorship or bright prospects. You should not be an equity investor unless you understand the magnitude and structure of these risks, and are prepared to live with them.

Living with stock market risk has a two-fold interpretation—investors must be able to live with stock market risk both financially and psychologically. From a financial point of view, investors must know what they will do if, for some unfortunate reason, their portfolios drop 20 percent or 30 percent or 50 percent or more. If they have other resources which can provide for their economic support until their stock market investments recover, if ever, they may be justified in incurring the risks.

The psychological aspects of risk are equally important. Some people can't sleep nights for fear of what might happen to their investments. Others are constantly badgered by their friends, their boss, or their spouse because of a bad investment or two. Psychological costs can add substantially to the financial costs of incurring stock market risk, and one or the other or both may make the whole not worthwhile. This is an individual decision to which there are no easy answers. The financial risks can be outlined a bit more graphically, but the psychological risks are completely up to individual temperament.

Consequently, risk analysis is very important. Investors need to decide the degree of risk exposure they can assume *before* they get involved in particular investments. Then the risks of a potential investment need to be carefully evaluated before action is taken. Is that investment likely to provide sufficient returns to justify the risk? And, even if it does qualify on the basis of risk and return, is that investment risk appropriate for my portfolio? Is it too risky, or risky enough? And, how does it affect diversification? These are critical stock market questions to which modern investment techniques can be addressed.

WHY TAKE RISKS?

A simple question—why take risks? A simple and correct answer—to earn a higher return on your investments. The positive relationship between risk and return is one of the few scientifically verified aspects of finance. Consider a few simple illustrations. U.S. government bonds are normally considered the safest investments available.[1] Corporate bonds of even the largest, most successful, and financially secure companies usually provide higher returns than government bonds. Corporate bonds are only slightly more risky, but this risk receives a higher return. Within corporates, higher-risk bonds (lower-quality ratings) provide higher yields to maturity than safer bonds. Once again, higher risk provides higher returns. In periods of financial uncertainty, the premium provided to holders of the higher-risk bonds can be substantial, several percent per year, all as compensation for taking the extra risk of owning less secure investments.

Common stocks are more risky than bonds so one should expect common stocks to provide even higher returns. This has been true historically. Studies of the returns earned from various investment alternatives over several decades confirm that the financial markets have paid premiums to the holders of more risky assets. The results of one study are summarized as follows:

Return (percent per annum) 1926 to 1973*	
S&P 500 index of common stocks	9.3
Long-term bonds	3.6
Treasury bills	2.2
Inflation	2.0

*SOURCE: Ibbotson and Sinquefeld, "Seminar on the Analysis of Security Prices, May 1974," *Stocks, Bonds, Bills and Inflation*, Part 1, University of Chicago, Chicago, p. 122.

[1] U.S. governments are the safest from the point of view of U.S. investors. Foreign investors face the added problem of currency risk.

MEASURING RISK

It is helpful to quantify the trade-off between risk and expected return. Rates of return are already quantified, as they are simply percentages per year. It remains to assign a numerical scale to the risk parameter. If we assign the asset with the least risk, U.S. Treasury bills, as zero on our risk scale, and the stock market as, arbitrarily, unity on our risk scale, we have the makings of a risk measurement scheme. Essentially, what we are doing is assuming the safest available asset, U.S. Treasury bills, has no risk. Then we are assigning one unit on our scale as equivalent to the risk in the stock market. Thus, an asset at 1.0 on the risk scale would have the same risk as the stock market, an asset with a risk of 0.5 on our risk scale would have one-half the risk of the stock market, and so forth.

RISK/RETURN DIAGRAM

Exhibit 4-1 is a graph of the trade-off between risk and return. The vertical axis is return and the horizontal axis is our risk scale, in units of stock market risk. Thus, the stock market appears at a rate of return of 9 percent and a risk of 1.0. Similarly, Treasury bills are shown with a return of 2 percent, the long-term historical rate, and a risk of zero, since compared to the stock market, Treasury bills have virtually no risk.

We hasten to add that the rates of return assigned to Treasury bills and the stock market in Exhibit 4-1 are arbitrarily set at the historical levels mentioned earlier. This is not a forecast of future returns. Indeed, with today's high interest rates, few would find a 2 percent return from Treasury bills at all acceptable. The rates of return in Exhibit 4-1 are for illustrative purposes only, and the reader is free to substitute his own projections.

In Exhibit 4-1, a dashed line has been drawn from the Treasury bill point through the stock market point. This is a particularly important line, called the capital market line in financial literature. Its interpretation is very simple. Each point on the line represents a portfolio partially in Treasury bills and partially in common stocks, that is, in the stock market. For example, a point on the line midway between Treasury bills and the stock market represents a portfolio which is 50 percent in Treasury bills and 50 percent in the stock market. This portfolio has a risk of 0.5 on our risk scale because it is halfway

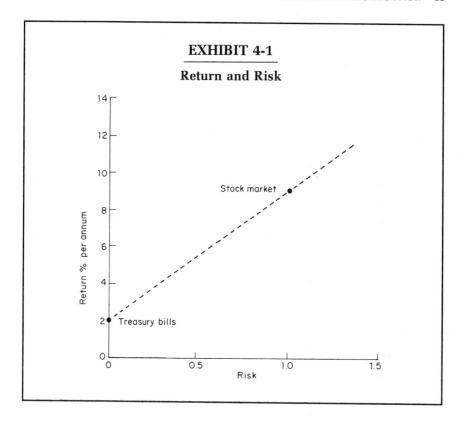

EXHIBIT 4-1

Return and Risk

between the 0.0 risk Treasury bills and the 1.0 risk stock market. The return expected from this portfolio is simply:

50 percent in bills at 2 percent	$= 0.5 \times 2\% = 1.0\%$
50 percent in stocks at 9 percent	$= 0.5 \times 9\% = 4.5\%$
For a total rate of return of	5.5%

The capital market line establishes the threshold of acceptable investments. Suppose someone offers you the opportunity of investing in an asset that provides a return of 7 percent but has the same risk as the stock market. Clearly, this is an inferior investment because its return is not comparable to its risk. For a risk of 1.0 on our risk scale, it provides only 7 percent return while the stock market itself provides 9 percent for the same level of risk. Why take 7 percent when 9 percent is readily available? Assets whose risk and return place them below the dashed line in Exhibit 4-1 are inferior, as they are dominated by the capital market line.

As a result, the capital market line defines the upper and lower limits of acceptable investments. In other words, almost every portfolio must fall somewhere on the capital market line. It cannot be above, that is, providing higher returns than the risk incurred, because market efficiency bids the prices of such investments up to where their returns are reduced to the capital market line. It cannot fall below the capital market line because no well-managed portfolio would invest so unwisely.

The capital market line does show why investors are willing to take risk. Over the long term, the capital markets pay premium returns to those willing and able to bear risk. These extra returns have been substantial. Over the last few decades, the premium to the stock market has been about 7 percentage points per annum over Treasury bills. And, 7 percent per annum compounded over many years can make a very great contribution to wealth. To achieve this extra return, investors must be able, financially and psychologically, to hold risky assets for long periods of time, literally decades. Not every investor is able to, and not every investor should.

The capital market line encompasses a wide spectrum of risks, from Treasury bills to assets far more risky than the stock market. And every investment portfolio, whether it be high-flying stocks or safe bonds, must fall on that line. The selection of the point on the line appropriate to a particular investor, the risk and return trade-off most suitable to him, is very important. This selection requires a greater understanding of the nature of risk, where various assets stand on the risk-return trade-off, and how assets combine into diversified portfolios.

RISK AS FLUCTUATION IN VALUE

To most investors, risk means how much can be lost, how far a stock can go down. Obviously, no one invests with the expectation that his stock will go down. But we always realize that unforeseen events can have a negative impact on the value of our holdings. Loss is always possible, and we would like to know something about the magnitude of that possible loss before we invest.

Magnitude of possible loss is most difficult to evaluate. Most of the tools investors use to evaluate potential loss, such as what is the lowest price/earnings ratio (P/E) this stock can sell at, or at what price would the stock's dividend yield provide support, do not work very well. In recent bear markets, too many stocks have dropped to new lows, far below their previous lowest P/E and providing much higher yields than anyone foresaw. Many investors have learned the hard way that a stock selling at a new low price or a new low P/E or a high yield not seen since the 1950s still has plenty of risk. It can still go lower.

It is more helpful to think of risk as how much the price of a stock is likely to fluctuate, how much it is likely to move in either direction, not just down but up as well. It is axiomatic that stocks which move up very rapidly are capable of moving down just as quickly. So the degree of fluctuation in both directions, up or down, is a helpful guide to risk.

This can be seen by evaluating the annual price range of familiar stocks. Exhibit 4-2 shows the high price, low price, and range of IBM for each year from 1968 to 1975. Range is calculated simply as high price minus low price divided by average price, and expressed as a percentage. That is:

$$\text{Range} = 100\% \times \frac{\text{high} - \text{low}}{(\text{high} + \text{low})/2}$$

EXHIBIT 4-2

IBM Stock Price 1968 to 1975
(All prices adjusted for stock splits through 1975)

	High Price	Low Price	Percent Range
1968	$300.00	$224.00	29.0
1969	294.90	233.30	23.3
1970	309.60	175.00	55.6
1971	292.50	226.50	25.4
1972	341.30	265.30	25.1
1973	365.13	235.13	43.3
1974	254.00	150.50	51.2
1975	227.38	157.25	36.5
		AVERAGE	36.2

$$\text{Range} = 100\% \times \frac{\text{high} - \text{low}}{(\text{high} + \text{low})/2}$$

EXHIBIT 4-3

National Semiconductor Stock Price 1968 to 1975
(All prices adjusted for splits through 1975)

	High Price	Low Price	Percent Range
1968	$ 8.42	$5.00	50.9
1969	11.33	7.00	47.3
1970	9.42	1.92	132.4
1971	6.88	3.08	76.2
1972	13.21	6.50	68.1
1973	36.25	7.63	130.5
1974	25.13	6.25	120.3
1975	48.38	9.25	135.8
		AVERAGE	95.2

$$\text{Range} = 100\% \times \frac{\text{high} - \text{low}}{(\text{high} + \text{low})/2}$$

EXHIBIT 4-4

Annual Percentage Ranges for 10 Popular Stocks
(In ascending order)

	1968	1969	1970	1971
Exxon	24.4	34.3	38.1	20.6
IBM	29.0	23.3	55.6	25.4
General Motors	21.2	24.0	31.1	21.6
Florida Light & Power	24.3	17.0	32.3	30.2
Citicorp	43.7	35.2	30.4	36.0
Xerox	35.7	35.4	55.8	39.7
American Express	50.4	21.1	50.1	51.0
UAL	64.7	60.0	77.7	71.9
MGIC	91.7	34.1	70.1	70.9
National Semiconductor	50.9	47.3	132.4	76.2

IBM's annual price range had a low of about 23 percent in 1967 and was about 25 percent in 1971 and 1972. On the other hand, the range reached a maximum in the bear market year of 1970 at a value of 55.6 percent. IBM has provided handsome returns to those investors who have owned it over the last several decades. But IBM has considerable risk in that its stock price range can be over 50 percent in a single year. The average annual range for this 6-year period is 36.2 percent.

Exhibit 4-3 shows the same data for National Semiconductor Corporation. National Semiconductor is a smaller, rapidly growing company in a very dynamic field. Its stock price has been very volatile. Its safest year, if we can use that expression, was 1969, when the annual stock price percentage range was only 47 percent. Compare this with IBM's *widest* range of 55 percent. National Semiconductor's maximum annual range was 136 percent in 1975, with 1970's 132 percent and 1973's 130 percent not far behind. The average annual range for National Semiconductor has been 95 percent, compared to IBM's 36 percent. It is easy to see how National Semiconductor earned its reputation as a volatile security.

Exhibit 4-4 shows the annual ranges for 10 popular stocks. IBM is

1972	1973	1974	1975	Avg.
27.0	20.7	58.0	36.5	32.5
25.1	43.3	51.2	36.5	36.2
17.3	61.4	63.1	61.1	37.6
45.3	51.9	73.7	53.4	41.0
56.4	42.0	75.6	44.7	45.8
35.1	38.8	88.7	60.1	48.6
41.0	50.3	92.4	58.1	51.8
61.2	76.7	78.7	70.6	70.2
73.9	120.6	153.4	82.4	87.1
68.1	130.5	120.3	135.8	95.2

among the safest in this group, exceeded only by Exxon. National Semiconductor is the riskiest but MGIC and UAL (formerly United Airlines) are almost as volatile. Of course, many other widely held stocks are as volatile as these three.

Even the most popular stocks have considerable volatility. They can go up or down by significant percentages in a single year and by larger amounts over longer time periods. The range calculation gives a fairly good index of the relative riskiness of the various stocks. Most investors know that National Semiconductor, UAL, and similar stocks are among the more volatile. This simple numerical calculation of risk, annual range, coincides with our experience with these stocks.

Range as a measure of risk emphasizes an important point. Risk is how much a stock can go up as well as how much it can go down. Some of these annual range percentages were made when stocks started the year at a high level and fell, the standard view of risk. In other years, stocks started low and went up through the year. What goes up a lot can come down a lot. In that sense, some of our return is really evidence of riskiness, while some of the risk we experience as prices fall is evidence of potential return.

RISK AS DISPERSION

We have seen so far that risk has to do with the degree to which stock prices can move in either direction. Rapid advances in stock price are just as indicative of risk as the sudden declines we all fear. We have evaluated risk by the annual range of stock price, wide ranges implying high risk.

Annual ranges in stock prices are the result of many, many smaller moves over shorter periods of time. The risk difference between IBM and National Semiconductor can also be illustrated by the weekly price changes of each stock. Since National Semiconductor is the more volatile security, we would expect its weekly price movements, expressed in percentage terms, to show much wider dispersion than IBM's. Exhibit 4-5 demonstrates that this is indeed the case. Exhibit 4-5 shows the dispersion of weekly price changes for IBM and National Semiconductor over a six-year period. In most of these weeks IBM's weekly percentage price change was between +4 and −4 percent. During this period, IBM never dropped more than 8 percent in a single week, and it never gained more than 12 percent in a single week.

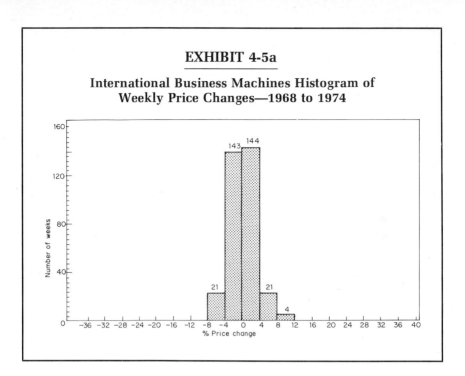

EXHIBIT 4-5a

International Business Machines Histogram of Weekly Price Changes—1968 to 1974

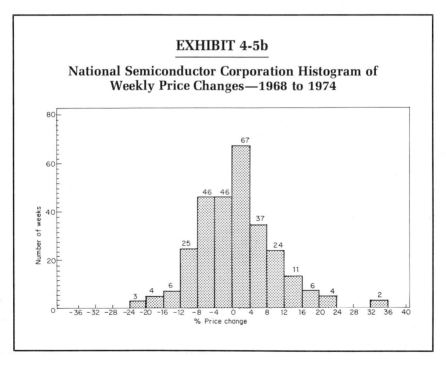

EXHIBIT 4-5b

National Semiconductor Corporation Histogram of Weekly Price Changes—1968 to 1974

National Semiconductor is a much different story. National Semiconductor's weekly price changes show much, much wider dispersion. True, there were many weeks when National Semiconductor's stock price was relatively stable, moving less than 4 percent in either direction. But National Semiconductor's stock price dropped more than 12 percent in 38 of these weeks. That is, National Semiconductor's shareholders lost at least 12 percent of their value more frequently than one week in 10. Similarly, large recoveries were relatively frequent. There were two weeks in this period when National Semiconductor gained more than 30 percent. Single week gains greater than 8 to 10 percent were frequent.

Statisticians have a measure of dispersion that is helpful in risk measurement. This measure is called "standard deviation," which means simply the dispersion that a phenomenon is likely to display. The mathematical formula for standard deviation can be found in any basic statistical textbook and is not of concern to us here. However, using that formula, we find that IBM's weekly price changes have a standard deviation of 2.94 percent and National Semiconductor 8.94 percent. In other words, IBM's risk is about 3 percent and National Semiconductor's about 9 percent. National Semiconductor is about three times as risky as IBM. Its price fluctuations are about three times as volatile as IBM's, so National Semiconductor shareholders should expect to make and lose money about three times as fast as IBM shareholders.

Standard deviation as a measure of risk can be applied to the stock market as a whole. To illustrate, the S&P 500 stock index has been charted in Exhibit 4-6. The dispersion of weekly percentage changes in the S&P 500 index looks much more like the chart for IBM than for National Semiconductor. In fact, the dispersion of the S&P 500 is somewhat smaller than the dispersion for IBM. Using the statistician's measure of dispersion again, the S&P 500 has a dispersion of about 2.0 percent, somewhat below IBM's 2.9 percent and much, much less than National Semiconductor.

Comparing the dispersion of a stock's price changes with the stock market as a whole, in this case measured by the S&P 500, provides a means of stating the risk of each company. If we use the dispersion (standard deviation) of the market (S&P 500) as a basic unit of measure, we can express the risks of the other stocks on a comparable basis. We call this measure the "total risk" of a particular stock. The following table illustrates the calculation of total risk:

	(1) Standard Deviation	(2) Standard Deviation of S&P 500	(1)/(2) Total Risk
IBM	2.94	1.98	1.48
National Semiconductor	8.94	1.98	4.52
S&P 500	1.98	1.98	1.00

To review, we have defined the stock market, in this case the S&P 500, as having a total risk of 1.0. This establishes a unit of measure of risk and provides a scale against which the risk of other investments can be compared. On this scale, IBM is 48 percent more risky than the S&P 500. That is, an investment in IBM alone with no other assets to provide diversification is 48 percent more risky than owning a very broadly diversified portfolio, that is, the market. Similarly, owning just National Semiconductor has 4½ times as much risk or as much price fluctuation as owning the S&P 500.

Total risk illustrates the considerable fluctuation in value inherent in all stocks. This is a natural, even necessary, part of the stock market. If

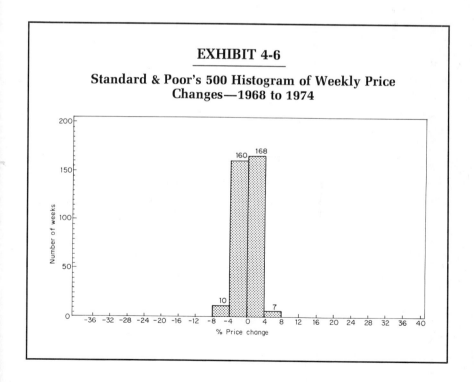

EXHIBIT 4-6

Standard & Poor's 500 Histogram of Weekly Price Changes—1968 to 1974

it were not for this fluctuation in value, this risk, there would be no reason to expect these investments to provide higher rates of return than very safe assets such as Treasury bills. The capital markets are paying a premium in expected return to investors willing to bear this risk, to subject their assets to this fluctuation in value. The capital markets are saying, in effect, that if you are willing to bear this risk, you can expect a higher rate of return. You may not get it. Risk may work against you, and you may lose. But, on average and over long periods of time, you should expect to earn a premium return for bearing risk.

THE COMPONENTS OF RISK

We have already seen that the stock market, in this case the S&P 500 stock index, has less total risk or total dispersion than most stocks. This is an empirical phenomenon. Experience has shown that a well-diversified portfolio, and owning all the stocks in the market is certainly well diversified, is less risky than owning one or a handful of securities. The reason for this will now be explored.

Individual stock prices change for two primary reasons. First, the stock market itself may go up or down, and this is likely to have an impact on a particular stock. If the stock market falls precipitously because of some item of news that is particularly bad, most stocks will fall as well. In market rallies, most stocks will respond favorably. In fact, in strong bull markets, almost every stock will benefit; and, in severe bear markets, only a handful of stocks will avoid declines.

Yet no stock performs exactly in line with the market. On any given day, some stocks make new highs and some new lows, no matter whether the market is up or down. News unique to particular stocks can cause their prices to rise or fall to some extent independent of the market. If IBM reports some particularly favorable event on a day the market is off because of bad economic or political news, IBM may rally while the market averages are down, or vice versa.

No stock is a perfect mimic of the market and no stock is totally immune to the market. All stock prices are affected by two factors—the market and a component unique to themselves. Sometimes these two components act in concert, driving the stock price up or down by significant amounts; at other times, these two components act contrary to one another, negating each other's effect. But the two components— a market component and a unique component—are always there.

These components can be measured and analyzed and provide significant insight into the riskiness of a particular stock and the functioning of diversification.

Exhibit 4-7 shows how the two components of price movement interact in the case of IBM. One column in the table is the weekly percentage changes in price for IBM. These were shown in graph form in the bell-shaped curve in Exhibit 4-5.

Another column shows the same information for the S&P 500 stock average. A quick visual review of these two columns again illustrates the points we made previously. IBM tends to move up and down with somewhat larger swings than the S&P 500. Both are capable of significant up and down moves. Recall that these are percentage changes in value in a single week. The stock market fluctuates on a weekly basis by amounts comparable to returns one could expect to earn in a savings account or Treasury bills in months or even a year or more.

Exhibit 4-7 also demonstrates that IBM and the S&P 500 often move in the same direction. This occurred in 36 of the 52 weeks shown in the exhibit, and the sample period, 1973, is no doubt typical of other times as well. But IBM does not usually move up or down by the same magnitude as the S&P 500; IBM usually does somewhat better or somewhat worse than the S&P 500, with no apparent pattern on a weekly basis as to how much better or worse. Again, this illustrates the two components of price fluctuation—the overall market and factors unique to the stock—and their impact on IBM. Each component will now be analyzed.

MARKET RISK

Financial research has developed a helpful approach to measuring the impact of the market on a particular stock or portfolio. This is usually called the "beta" factor in financial jargon, but we shall use the term "market risk." The determination of beta or market risk is demonstrated in Exhibit 4-8. Here two items from Exhibit 4-7, the percentage price change of IBM and the percentage change in the S&P 500, have been plotted on the vertical and horizontal axes, respectively. A given point in the diagram indicates what IBM and the S&P 500 did in a particular week in 1973. The diagonal line in Exhibit 4-8 is a best-fitting line through the data points. (Actually, it's through the points on another chart covering even more years of data.) The diagonal line

EXHIBIT 4-7

International Business Machines

Year/Week	S&P Price	S&P Pct Chg	IBM Stock Price	IBM Stock Pct Chg
73 01	118.05	1.92	321.60	2.94
73 02	119.87	1.54	335.00	4.17
73 03	119.30	−0.48	336.00	0.30
73 04	118.78	−0.44	351.20	4.52
73 05	116.45	−1.96	350.20	−0.28
73 06	114.35	−1.80	343.80	−1.83
73 07	114.68	0.29	356.80	3.78
73 08	114.98	0.26	353.00	−1.07
73 09	113.16	−1.58	346.80	−1.76
73 10	112.28	−0.78	353.60	1.96
73 11	114.55	2.02	351.60	−0.57
73 12	113.54	−0.88	354.80	0.91
73 13	108.88	−4.10	342.40	−3.49
73 14	111.52	2.42 ·	345.20	0.82
73 15	109.28	−2.01	338.80	−1.85
73 16	112.08	2.56	343.80	1.48
73 17	112.17	0.08	343.20	−0.17
73 18	107.23	−4.40	324.20	−5.54
73 19	111.00	3.52	337.40	4.07
73 20	108.17	−2.55	324.50	−3.82
73 21	103.86	−3.98	311.20	−4.10
73 22	107.94	3.93	326.40	4.88
73 23	103.93	−3.72	310.00	−5.02
73 24	107.03	2.98	324.25	4.60
73 25	105.10	−1.80	318.25	−1.85
73 26	103.70	−1.33	316.75	−0.47
73 27	104.62	0.89	317.00	0.08

Year/Week	S&P Price	S&P Pct Chg	IBM Stock Price	IBM Stock Pct Chg
73 28·	101.28	−3.19	300.25	−5.28
73 29	104.09	2.77	310.00	3.25
73 30	107.14	2.93	315.00	1.61
73 31	109.59	2.29	318.00	0.95
73 32	106.49	−2.83	311.50	−2.04
73 33	104.77	−1.62	301.25	−3.29
73 34	102.31	−2.35	300.50	−0.25
73 35	101.62	−0.67	298.25	−0.75
73 36	104.25	2.59	301.00	0.92
73 37	104.76	0.49	296.12	−1.62
73 38	104.44	−0.31	298.00	0.63
73 39	107.20	2.64	260.00	−12.75
73 40	108.43	1.15	258.00	−0.77
73 41	109.85	1.31	259.50	0.58
73 42	111.44	1.45	282.00	8.67
73 43	110.22	−1.09	291.50	3.37
73 44	111.38	1.05	285.50	−2.06
73 45	107.07	−3.87	280.25	−1.84
73 46	105.30	−1.65	278.37	−0.67
73 47	103.88	−1.35	284.50	2.20
73 48	99.44	−4.27	272.50	−4.22
73 49	95.96	−3.50	265.00	−2.75
73 50	96.51	0.57	265.00	0.0
73 51	93.29	−3.34	246.00	−7.17
73 52	93.54	0.27	240.50	−2.24

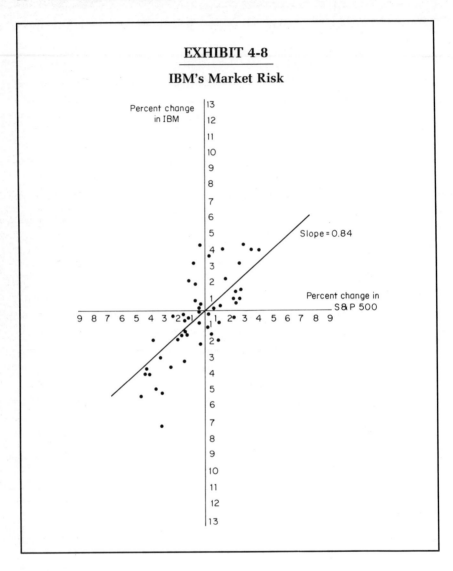

EXHIBIT 4-8

IBM's Market Risk

represents the average impact of the market on IBM, that is, the average change in IBM for each 1 percent change in the market.

The slope of this line happens to be 0.84, which means that IBM, on average, tends to move up 0.84 percent whenever the market rallies 1.0 percent and IBM tends to drop 0.84 percent whenever the market declines 1.0 percent. IBM tends to dampen moves in the market, to move less than the market. If the market should rally 10 percent, IBM would likely rally only 8.4 percent; or if the market should decline 20 percent, IBM would likely decline only 0.84 × 20 percent, or 16.8 percent. From the viewpoint of beta or market risk, IBM is less volatile than the market as IBM tends to understate moves in the market.

UNIQUE RISK

This is not the whole story for IBM, however. We have already seen that as far as total price fluctuation is concerned, IBM is more volatile than the market. This extra volatility comes from the component of risk that is unique to IBM, independent of the stock market as a whole. This unique component of risk is readily apparent in Exhibit 4-8. There is a rough correspondence between IBM and the market in that the sloping line fits the data points to an extent. But most points do not fall on the sloping line. They are dispersed around the line since, in any particular week, IBM usually does better or worse than might be expected from the stock market's effect alone. This dispersion around the sloping line follows another bell-shaped curve not unlike Exhibit 4-5 and represents the unique component of risk. Just as the total dispersion of IBM's stock price (Exhibit 4-5) can be measured by a standard deviation, this unique component of risk can be measured in a similar manner.

In summary, we have labeled the overall price fluctuation of a particular stock as total risk. This can be measured as a standard deviation or typical range of fluctuation and expressed in units of the stock market's fluctuation. Total risk or total price fluctuation can be divided into two components—a stock market component and a component unique to each stock. Market risk is the average impact of the stock market as a whole on a particular stock. This is determined by the slope of the line of best fit as in Exhibit 4-8. Of course, stocks usually perform somewhat better or poorer than market risk alone would indicate, since they fluctuate on their own above and beyond the impact of the market. This component is called unique risk or residual risk.

RISK TRIANGLE

Total risk and its two components can be conveniently charted in a so-called "risk triangle." The triangle shows how market risk and unique risk interact to cause total risk, the total price fluctuation in a particular stock. The risk triangle appears as follows:

Market risk and unique risk are drawn perpendicular to one another to illustrate their independence. One has no impact on the other. The two combine to cause total risk, the total price fluctuation in a particular stock. The combination is not directly additive but works in the sense of the Pythagorean theorem from high school geometry, that is,

$$(\text{Total risk})^2 = (\text{market risk})^2 + (\text{unique risk})^2$$

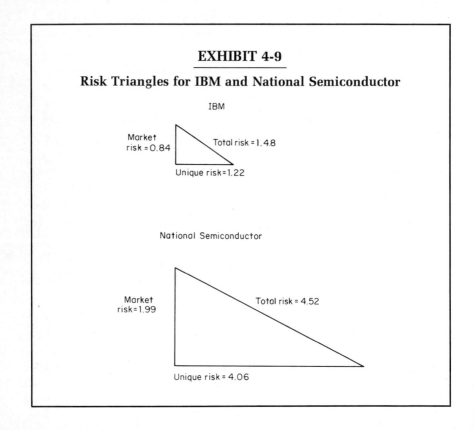

EXHIBIT 4-9

Risk Triangles for IBM and National Semiconductor

The risk triangle can be used to illustrate the vast differences in risk between our two example stocks, IBM and National Semiconductor. In Exhibit 4-9, risk triangles for both stocks have been drawn to scale so their sizes are indicative of relative risk. As we have already seen, National Semiconductor has much the greater total risk, shown on the hypotenuse of the triangle. This extra risk comes in part from greater market risk, 1.99 versus IBM's 0.84, but more importantly from greater unique risk. National Semiconductor is very sensitive to the market—it has a tendency to amplify market moves by two—but even more of its volatility comes from its tendency to fluctuate over and above the effect of the market by very considerable amounts.

In fact, on the basis of these risk triangles, one might almost wonder why the concept of market risk has been introduced. It appears, particularly for National Semiconductor, that market risk is by far the lesser of the two components of risk. Since in most cases, total risk and unique risk are similar in magnitude, should we not concentrate our attention on the major component, unique risk, or even ignore the two components and worry about total risk alone?

DIVERSIFICATION AND THE RISK TRIANGLE

This is where diversification comes into play and has an effect that is contrary to intuition. Diversification, the strategy of spreading investments over several alternative assets, tends to reduce risk by reducing unique risk. In a diversified portfolio, the unique risk components of the individual stocks tend to average out, to offset one another. On a day that the market is up, some stocks will be up more than the market and others less because of their unique risk. Some more and some less add up to almost nothing. Consequently, diversified portfolios tend to act like the market.

To illustrate this phenomenon, Exhibit 4-10 shows the risk triangle as more and more diversification is introduced into a hypothetical portfolio. First, with a single stock, the market risk and unique risk legs of the triangle are in about the same proportions as for IBM and National Semiconductor. Then, a second stock of about the same risk characteristics as the first is added to the portfolio. The two stocks combined have about the same market risk as the first stock, but the unique risk of the portfolio is reduced. The reason is that on some days when the first stock is beating the market, the second stock is underperforming. On other days, the second stock is pulling ahead, but the first is lagging. Of course, there are a few days when both stocks beat the

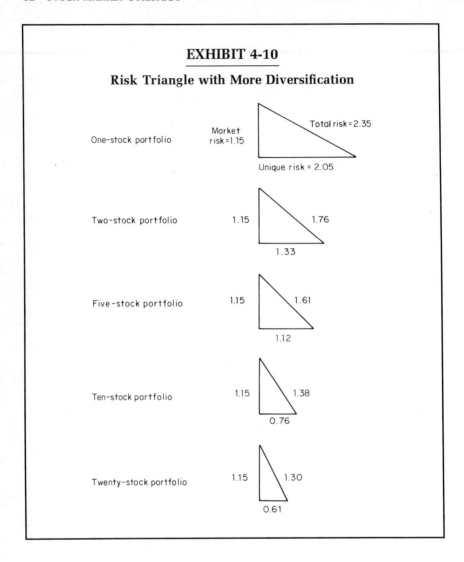

EXHIBIT 4-10

Risk Triangle with More Diversification

One-stock portfolio — Market risk =1.15 — Total risk =2.35 — Unique risk = 2.05

Two-stock portfolio — 1.15 — 1.76 — 1.33

Five-stock portfolio — 1.15 — 1.61 — 1.12

Ten-stock portfolio — 1.15 — 1.38 — 0.76

Twenty-stock portfolio — 1.15 — 1.30 — 0.61

market—but not nearly as many days as the one stock does. Similarly, there are a few days when both stocks underperform the market, but not nearly as many as when one stock underperforms. As a result, the total risk of the portfolio of two stocks is less than the single stock's total risk.

Exhibit 4-10 shows the result as more and more stocks are added to a portfolio. By the time a 20-stock portfolio is reached, that is, assets invested equally in 20 stocks, total risk has dropped substantially.

Total risk is now about 50 percent of what it was for a single stock. Diversification can have a very dramatic effect on reducing portfolio risk.

Market risk has not changed. The market risk of the portfolio is the average market risk of the individual stocks (weighted by the market value held in each stock). Diversification did nothing to reduce market risk. Indeed, a more and more diversified portfolio tends to look more and more like the market. Our definition of the market is simply the total of all the stocks traded on the exchange. As more and more stocks are added to a portfolio, the portfolio begins to act more and more like the overall market.

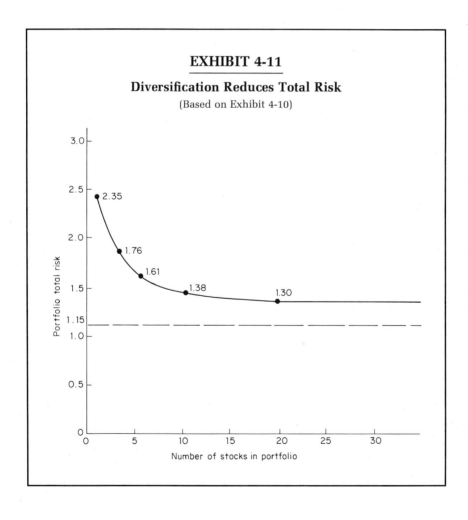

EXHIBIT 4-11

Diversification Reduces Total Risk

(Based on Exhibit 4-10)

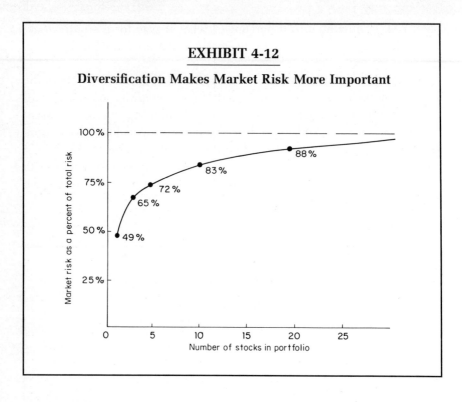

EXHIBIT 4-12

Diversification Makes Market Risk More Important

The rapidity with which a portfolio approximates the market may be surprising. With a perfectly diversified portfolio, all unique risk is eliminated and the portfolio's risk consists solely of market risk. Our 20-stock portfolio had already reduced its unique risk to such an extent that the total risk of the portfolio was dominated by market risk. (Market risk was nearly 90 percent of total risk.) In this case, it required only 20 stocks to have about the same risk characteristics as the 500 stocks in the S&P 500. It only takes a few stocks to make a well-diversified portfolio, that is, a portfolio whose performance is dominated by the performance of the overall stock market. This phenomenon is illustrated in Exhibits 4-11 and 4-12.

IMPLICATIONS FOR INVESTORS

Diversification is extremely important. Owning a portfolio of one or two or a handful of stocks is very risky. This applies as well to portfolios of many stocks where the market value of the portfolio is dominated by one or two large holdings. Such portfolios are underdiversified and subject to far more risk than need be incurred. This extra risk may have helped these portfolios do well in the past, but they can go down rapidly as well. Since even 20 stocks of varying types from several industries can provide reasonably good diversification, there is no need for overconcentration.

Diversification, in turn, increases a portfolio's dependence on the performance of the stock market as a whole. Consequently, forecasting the stock market is extremely important to investment success. The market is the dominant component of the risk of a diversified portfolio because market risk cannot be diversified away. Thus, portfolios are likely to mimic moves in the overall market. If the market rallies, the portfolio is likely to provide a favorable return. So market forecasting and being invested at the proper times are very critical, far more critical than most investors realize.

This suggests the importance of time diversification. Since one is never certain which way the market will go next—even sophisticated systems for market timing have considerable room for error—one should diversify with respect to time. If you are investing, you will reduce your risk by investing slowly, perhaps over many months or longer. If the market drops, you will get some of your investments at lower prices. On the other hand, if the market rallies, you may want to be patient and slow your buying until a decline comes along. In any case, time diversification is as important as diversifying over holdings.

Since market risk cannot be diversified out of a portfolio of stocks, investors should be wary of an investment program totally dependent on the success of the stock market. Other assets may have lower market risk, no market risk, or even negative market risk. For example, the values of long-term bonds are somewhat related to the stock market, but they have less market risk than most stocks and thereby provide some diversification not available in the stock market. Treasury bills or other short-term liquid assets have essentially no market risk, so they can substantially reduce the risk of a portfolio. Some gold mining stocks even have negative market risk. They may move up when the stock market is weak and may perform poorly when the stock market is strong. While these assets need to be evaluated on their own, they potentially have the benefit of substantially reducing the market risk of a portfolio, thereby reducing overall risk. In some cases, this risk reduction may be so beneficial as to warrant inclusion of these assets in a portfolio even though their returns may not be particularly exciting on their own merits.

HOW RISKY IS YOUR PORTFOLIO?

We now turn to the most crucial questions—how risky is your portfolio, and how risky should your portfolio be? The modern capital theory techniques that have been introduced will prove very helpful in answering these questions. We can do the best job of telling you how risky your portfolio—your current portfolio or a portfolio you are considering—really is. Exhibit 4-13 lists the approximate risk parameters of the more popular securities investments. We say approximate because individual stocks and bonds can differ from these aggregate statistics. The numbers are only to indicate midpoints of a range or spectrum of risks. For example, many top quality industrial stocks have market risks of 1.0, about equal to the stock market as a whole as measured by the S&P 500. Some, of course, will be less than 1.0 and some more, but as a rule of thumb, using market risk of 1.0 for the lot is reasonable.

Both market risk and total risk are shown in Exhibit 4-13 because of the differences resulting from various levels of diversification. The risk of a single asset alone is much different from the risk contribution that asset makes to a diversified portfolio. Standing alone, total risk should be used. As part of a portfolio, market risk is the appropriate measure.

EXHIBIT 4-13

Approximate Risk Parameters of Typical Investments

	Market Risk	Total Risk
US Treasury bills	0	0
Top-quality commercial paper	0+	0+
Long-term government bonds	0.3	0.6
Long-term corporate bonds	0.4	0.7
Diversified common stock portfolio (S&P 500)	1.0	1.0
A single utility stock	0.6	1.5
A single top-quality industrial stock	1.0	2.5
A single aggressive stock	2.0	5.0
A single gold stock	−0.1	2.0

Recall that National Semiconductor has a huge total risk, 4.5 times that of the S&P 500 index. An investor whose total assets are tied up in that stock is going to have very volatile investment results, making and losing large portions of his wealth in short periods of time. On the other hand, as part of a diversified portfolio, National Semiconductor's risk contribution is "only" 2.0 times the risk of the S&P 500.

Similarly, an advocate of gold investments, a "gold bug," might at some point have a large proportion of assets in gold stocks. By concentrating his assets, he is taking extra risk, on the order of twice an investment in top-quality industrial common stocks. His total wealth will change quickly, possibly in his favor and possibly against him. However, if only a portion of his assets are in gold and the rest diversified in other assets, the result is very different. Here, market risk is the appropriate measure of risk. Market risk for gold stocks can actually be negative due to gold stocks' tendency to move contrary to the stock market. Thus, a small investment in gold stocks can actually reduce the market risk and the total risk of a portfolio.

Using Exhibit 4-13, calculating the risk of a portfolio is straightforward. Consider a typical example: Doctor D, a retired general practitioner, has a portfolio consisting of:

> 20 percent in Treasury bills
> 20 percent in long government bonds
> 20 percent in long corporate bonds
> 35 percent in diversified common stocks
> 5 percent in gold stocks

The percentages represent the portion of the market value of his total assets in each category. The risk of his portfolio can be computed using Exhibit 4-13, weighting the market risk of each asset category by its market value percentage in Doctor D's portfolio. This is shown in the worksheet in Exhibit 4-14a. Using this worksheet, we find that Dr. D has a portfolio risk of 0.485 or slightly less than halfway between a riskless all-Treasury-bill portfolio and a 100 percent stock market portfolio. Since he is retired, this may very well be an appropriate risk level for him.

Ms. M, on the other hand, is a rising young business executive. She earns an excellent salary, has a company-funded retirement plan working for her, and can afford a more aggressive risk level in her investment portfolio. Her investment assets are:

EXHIBIT 4-14a

Dr. D's Portfolio Risk

Asset	(1) Market Risk (Exhibit 4-13)	(2) Fraction in This Asset	Risk Impact (1) × (2)
U.S. Treasury bills	0	0.20	0
Long governments	0.3	0.20	0.06
Long corporates	0.4	0.20	0.08
Diversified common stocks	1.0	0.35	0.35
Gold stocks	−0.1	0.05	−0.005
		Dr. D's portfolio risk	0.485

10 percent Treasury bills
40 percent several top-quality industrial stocks
50 percent several aggressive stocks

Her portfolio risk is calculated using the worksheet approach in Exhibit 4-14b. Once again market risk is used because she owns several stocks in each category, that is, her portfolio is diversified. If she had 50

EXHIBIT 4-14b

Ms. M's Portfolio Risk

Asset	(1) Market Risk (Exhibit 4-13)	(2) Fraction in This Asset	Risk Impact (1) × (2)
Treasury bills	0	.10	0
Top-quality industrials	1.0	.40	0.40
Aggressive stocks	2.0	.50	1.00
		Ms. M's portfolio risk	1.40

percent of her assets in just one aggressive stock, the total risk of 5.0 would have been used instead of the market risk of 2.0.

In any case, the resulting portfolio total risk of 1.40 is a fairly high number. It represents a great deal of risk which can result in very rapid profits or very rapid losses. While this portfolio may be appropriate for an aggressive young professional person with a positive outlook on the world, it is not a portfolio for the timid—which leads to the next risk question.

HOW MUCH RISK IS RIGHT FOR YOU?

How much risk is right for you? How much risk can you and your investment program tolerate? This is an intensely personal question that only you can answer. All that can be done is to advise you of the parameters of risk, the magnitude of the risks that you are taking, and provide some guidelines that may assist you to face the problem squarely.

Exhibit 4-15 shows the implications of risk. Risk is expressed at the bottom of the chart in units of S&P 500 risk. That is, 1.0 means the portfolio is taking the same risk as the S&P 500. A risk of 1.5 means the portfolio is taking 50 percent more risk than the S&P 500.

The vertical axis represents the returns that might be achieved in a given annual period. Note that the *average* line slopes upward to the right, as more risk provides more expected return. That means that 50 percent of the time your return should be above that line and 50 percent below that line.

The 5 percent, 25 percent, 75 percent, and 95 percent lines are also shown. Thus, if you take risk equivalent to the S&P 500, 5 percent of the time your annual return will fall below −25 percent. That is, in 1 year in 20, you will lose 25 percent. But you might get lucky and make 50 percent. That also happens about 1 year in 20. As you increase risk, your chances of bigger losses increase. But your chances of a big gain also improve. Keep in mind that only well-diversified portfolios have risks as low as 1.0. A single stock may have a total risk of four or five times as much. So the chances of huge losses and gigantic gains in a single stock are amplified accordingly.

One additional caveat of a technical nature. The analysis in Exhibit 4-15 assumes that stock price changes follow a particular probability distribution. Actually, stock prices fluctuate *more* than this. Thus, Exhibit 4-15 understates risk and should be interpreted as a lower bound on risk. Risks are at least as large as those described in the exhibit, and probably greater.

What does this mean for our friends Ms. M and Dr. D? Their risk exposure has been charted in Exhibit 4-16. The exhibit shows the range of returns that each might reasonably expect in an annual period. Dr. D

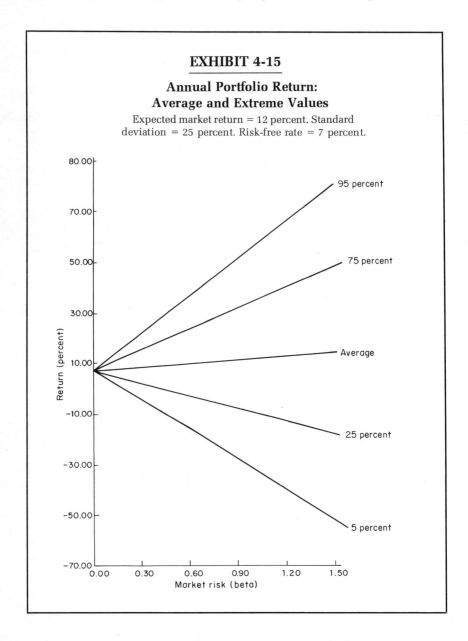

EXHIBIT 4-15

Annual Portfolio Return:
Average and Extreme Values

Expected market return = 12 percent. Standard
deviation = 25 percent. Risk-free rate = 7 percent.

could reasonably see a drop in his wealth of 10 percent or so. Or, he might have an excellent year and gain 30 percent. Ms. M has a much different situation. A decline in value in excess of 40 percent is a distinct possibility, as is a gain approaching 80 percent.

Since the line marked "Average" slopes upward to the right, Ms. M

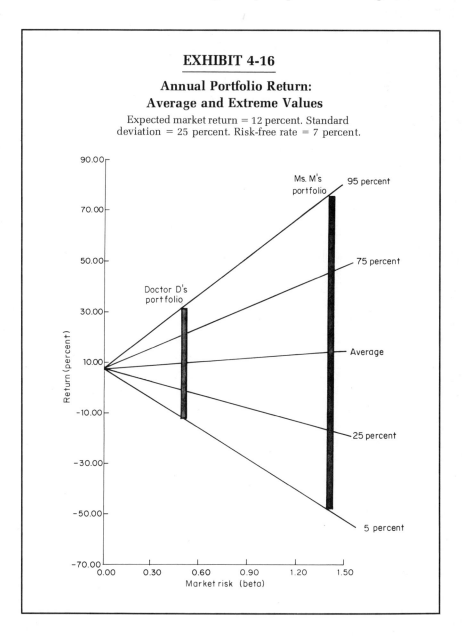

EXHIBIT 4-16

Annual Portfolio Return:
Average and Extreme Values

Expected market return = 12 percent. Standard
deviation = 25 percent. Risk-free rate = 7 percent.

has a higher expected return in compensation for her incurring a greater degree of risk. Whether or not the extra return potential is worth the risk is a question only she can answer. Basically, there are three key factors in this decision—the financial factor, the psychological factor, and the current market outlook. Financially, she may very well be able to afford this kind of risk. She is young with a secure current income and a pension plan program from her employer. She does not depend on her own investments for current income. Financially, she may be able to afford wide fluctuations in her total capital.

Psychological pressures are another factor. How does reading the morning paper and finding her assets have declined 10 percent on a bad day affect her life? If such news is upsetting, affecting her performance on her job and her attitude toward her friends and associates, she probably is incurring too much risk. Insomnia is an important clue to the level of risk an investor should incur in the stock market.

Third, the current outlook for the stock market must be considered. As we have already demonstrated, fluctuations in the stock market as a whole, as measured by the popular market averages, have a tremendous impact on portfolio values. While one or two or a handful of stocks may be able to move contrary to the market trend, most diversified portfolios have just as many who are adversely affected by the market. The losers have a tendency to cancel out the winners, leaving the overall market as the dominant influence on portfolio performance.

Market risk can be made to work for you. Most investors will want to increase the market risk of their portfolio when they are more optimistic on the outlook for the market. In turn, they will want to decrease the market risk of their portfolio when they are pessimistic on the outlook for the stock market. A conservative portfolio is appropriate for uncertain times just as a more aggressive portfolio can take advantage of a clearer, positive outlook. This is not to suggest that Dr. D, our retired friend, would ever have as risky a portfolio as the more aggressive Ms. M. But he might want to take a relatively more risky posture than usual if his outlook for the market is particularly favorable.

An investor must select an investment program consistent with his financial requirements, psychological comfort, and investment outlook. While there are no firm guidelines for decision, the actions of others may be a helpful clue. Exhibit 4-17 is a chart relating investment opportunities—various types of stocks, bonds, mutual funds, and Treasury bills—to common categories of investment objectives, ranging from conservative to speculators. Many conservative, income-oriented

EXHIBIT 4-17

Matching Investment Opportunities with Investor Categories.

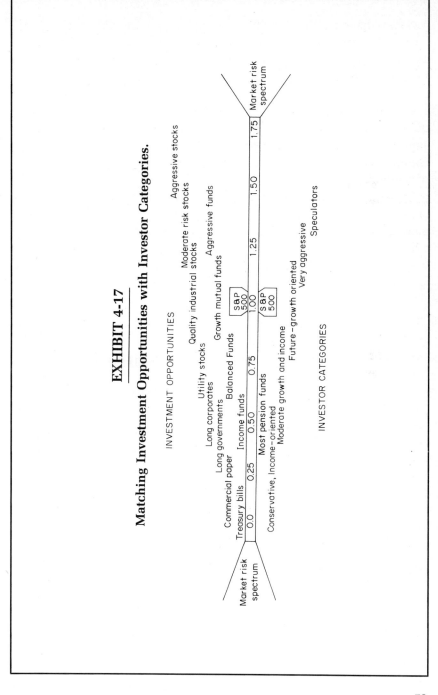

investors have portfolios with risk levels approximating that of long-term bonds. Of course, they may own long bonds or they can balance a common stock portfolio with safer Treasury bills, commercial paper, or savings accounts. From a risk point of view, the effect is about the same.

Growth-oriented investors, on the other hand, tend to concentrate their assets in common stocks. Again, keep in mind that balancing aggressive stocks with cash equivalent investments, Treasury bills, or commercial paper can average out to the risk equivalent of a portfolio of moderate quality stocks.

Exhibit 4-17 has no boundary to the right, to the high side of risk, because there is no upper limit to risk. Buying aggressive stocks on margin can double or triple the risk level. Call options are another vehicle for multiplying risk, providing leverage 8 or 10 or more times that of the S&P 500. While there is no effective upper limit on risk, few will want to swim in these treacherous waters.

EXHIBIT 4-18

Lower Risk Tendencies

Financial

1. Require high level of current investment income.
2. Investment capital critical to future income.
3. Unable to make up large losses from other income sources.
4. Nearing retirement age.

Psychological

1. You get investment insomnia.
2. Your peers criticize your investment mistakes.
3. You lack investment knowledge and experience.

Market Outlook

1. You are cautious about the investment outlook.

CONCLUSION

Risk is a vital investment subject. In a sense, risk is what the stock market is all about. Bearing risk is the reason that, over the long term, stock holders should expect returns substantially above the risk-free rate. Long-term studies of stock market returns verify this. However, there is no guarantee that you or I will succeed. Risk also means there is substantial opportunity for loss, even total disaster. Stock market risks are considerable. The stock market is a place where an investor can gain and lose a lot of money in a relatively short time. Many have.

How much risk should you take? The answer depends on your financial situation, your psychological state, and your outlook for the stock market. Exhibit 4-18 summarizes some of the factors you will want to consider in selecting a risk level appropriate for you. For convenience, the factors are listed under the financial, psychological, and outlook categories we have mentioned. This information can be a

Higher Risk Tendencies

Financial

. You have little or no need for current investment income.
. You can make up capital losses from other sources.
. You are investing for future needs, for growth.
. Your investments are small compared to your other income sources.
. You are relatively young.

Psychological

. You have a gambler's nerves.
. You are slow to react to adverse news, unlikely to overreact.
. You are a knowledgeable, informed, experienced investor.

Market Outlook

. You are relatively optimistic about the investment outlook.

helpful guide, but you must make the choice. It is one of the most important investment decisions you will ever make.

Finally, you should select a portfolio consistent with your risk tolerance. Every investment decision, every security trade, must be made in the light of this risk level. Many different combinations of assets can add up to a risk level appropriate for you. It is a matter of balancing the higher risk portion of your portfolio against the lower risk, to come up with the average you desire. The risk numbers in Exhibit 4-13 can be of assistance here, or you can obtain more precise numbers from your broker or investment advisor. These relatively simple calculations can provide invaluable guidance to your investment strategy.

FIVE

A Time to Buy, and a Time to Sell

THE IMPORTANCE OF MARKET TIMING

1973 was a bad year for those who doubt the value of market timing. The median decline of all common stocks listed on the New York Stock Exchange was over 32 percent. On the more volatile American Exchange, the median decline was a startling 46 percent. Assuming long-run average returns of about 9 percent per annum, these declines—not particularly severe by historical standards—were the equivalent of three or four years of normal market returns. That is, a holder of a typical stock might expect to wait several years just to get even.

Some investment analysts contend that stock selection is more important than market timing because in the long run good stocks will rebound from temporary market setbacks and provide superior returns. Without denying the importance of stock selection, it is clear that even the best stocks are unlikely to avoid market declines. Exhibit 5-1, for example, shows that only 18 percent of the stocks on the New York Stock Exchange avoided the 1973 decline. Less than one in five were up for the year. And the few winners were an exceptional breed that uniquely benefited from the troubled times.

While "grin and bear it" may provide some solace, it is clear that even the best stocks should not be held through severe market declines. Much better to dump them prior to the top, wait out the decline in a safe haven such as a savings account or commercial paper or Treasury

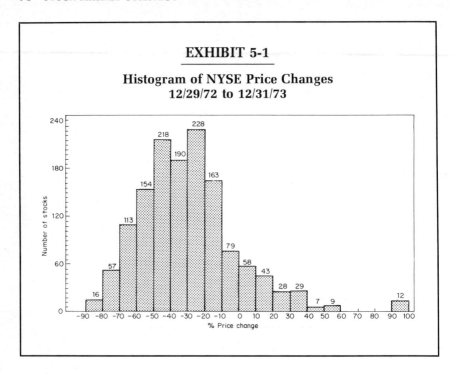

EXHIBIT 5-1

**Histogram of NYSE Price Changes
12/29/72 to 12/31/73**

bills, and buy those favorite stocks back at lower prices. In general, the strategy should be to try to hold good long-term stocks when they're going up and let someone else hold them when they're going down.

This does not imply frequent trading or portfolio churning. It is neither possible nor necessary to catch every minor turn in the market, or even to catch major turns right on the button. It does, however, mean that every couple of years or so one should make a really important decision about the beginning or ending of a bull market, and act accordingly. Consider these two examples:

Buy and Hold

Most investors would agree that IBM and Xerox have been sound long-term holdings, so-called "core growth" stocks. Look at their performance from the end of 1962 to the end of 1974, a 12-year period encompassing three major market advances (1962–65, 1966–68, and 1970–72) and three significant market declines (1966, 1969–70, and 1973–74). Over these 12 years, the annual compound rate of return, including price appreciation (adjusted for all stock splits) and dividends, was 7.7 percent on IBM and 14.8 percent on Xerox. For the entire S&P 500 stock price index, the figure was 4.0 percent. IBM and Xerox performed very well for their long-term holders over this period, beating the S&P 500 by 3.7 to 10.8 percentage points per annum (compounding even a 3.7 percent advantage for 12 years can amount to a significant sum). Overall, only a handful of stocks in the S&P 500 outperformed IBM and Xerox over this period.

Market Timing

Now consider market timing in the sense of catching most of the major turning points as an aid to investing in these two outstanding long-term holdings. Buying these stocks somewhere near market low points and selling them in the general vicinity of market highs can make a dramatic improvement in investment returns. Suppose one was skillful enough to:

- purchase these two stocks at the end of 1962 (The market low was in mid-1962.)

- sell out at the end of 1965 during a period of rampant speculative activity in the stock market

- buy back at the end of 1966 (three months after the market had bottomed and started to advance)

- sell again at the end of 1968 during another speculative boom

- buy for the third time at the end of 1970 (seven months after the market bottom in May 1970)

- sell for the third time at the end of 1972 (when the Dow Jones Industrial Average was surging above the 1,000 level for the first time)

Three buy decisions and three sell decisions in 12 years, each requiring some skill at market timing, are involved in this strategy. *Some* market timing skill is the appropriate description, because the strategy did not require selling at the precise market peak and did not require buying at the beginning of an advance. Rather, the strategy was to buy in the general area of market lows and sell in the general area of market tops, missing the best prices by modest margins.

What did this do for performance over the 12-year, 3-market cycle period? Exhibit 5-2 shows the calculations used to determine the results of the strategy. For simplicity, the calculations ignore trading costs (brokerage commissions, and so on) and assume only a 5 percent return on cash holdings when out of the market, though considerably higher rates were available. Taxes are also ignored. (In stock market timing, however, long-term capital gains taxes would have to be paid by most investors; in buy and hold, such taxes are deferred until sale.) The 12-year compound rates of return for the buy-and-hold and market-timing strategies over the 1962 to 1974 period compare as follows:

	Buy and Hold	*Some Market Timing*
IBM	7.70%	14.05%
Xerox	14.82%	28.12%
S&P 500	4.03%	11.12%

EXHIBIT 5-2a

IBM

(All prices and dividends adjusted for stock splits and distributions)

Year	Year End Price	Annual Dividend	Annual Percentage Return	Buy & Hold Cumulative Value Index	Market Timing Cumulative Value Index
1962	$ 81.17			100.00	100.00
1963	105.52	.88	31.1	131.10	131.10
1964	106.50	1.24	2.1	133.85	133.85
1965	129.82	1.56	23.4	165.17	165.17*
1966	144.93	1.68	12.9	186.48	173.43**
1967	250.80	1.74	74.2	324.85	302.11
1968	252.00	2.08	1.3	329.07	306.04*
1969	291.50	2.88	16.8	384.36	321.34
1970	254.10	3.84	−11.5	340.15	337.41**
1971	269.10	4.16	7.5	365.67	362.71
1972	321.60	4.32	21.1	442.82	439.25*
1973	246.75	4.48	−21.9	345.84	461.21
1974	168.00	6.00	−29.5	243.87	484.27

*Sell IBM, hold cash at 5% per annum.

**Buy IBM again.

Clearly, the difference is dramatic. Even modest market-timing skill, buying somewhere near the lows and selling somewhere near the highs, can make a dramatic contribution to overall returns from even the best long-term stock holdings. An investment of $1,000 left in Xerox for 12 years became $5,252. An excellent result. With a little timing it could have become $19,564. (See Exhibit 5-2b.) Growth stocks are great—but even the best of them take significant beatings in the market. Avoiding those declines, even partially, can significantly improve overall investment returns.

HOW TO TELL TIME: READING THE INDICATORS

Most investors acknowledge the advantages of buy low, sell high. But many doubt it is possible to determine that a market peak or bottom is

---

EXHIBIT 5-2b

Xerox

(All prices and dividends adjusted for stock splits and distributions)

Year	Year End Price	Annual Dividend	Annual Percentage Return	Buy & Hold Cumulative Value Index	Market Timing Cumulative Value Index
1962	$ 10.56			100.00	100.00
1963	28.83	.08	173.7	273.77	273.77
1964	32.88	.14	14.5	313.47	313.47
1965	67.33	.20	105.4	643.90	643.90*
1966	65.83	.28	−1.8	632.30	676.10**
1967	101.00	.40	54.0	973.70	1,041.20
1968	89.13	.50	−11.3	863.67	923.50*
1969	105.75	.65	19.4	1,031.20	969.70
1970	86.50	.65	−17.6	849.70	1,018.20**
1971	125.25	.80	45.7	1,238.10	1,483.50
1972	149.25	.84	19.8	1,483.20	1,777.20*
1973	122.75	.90	−17.2	1,228.10	1,866.10
1974	51.50	1.00	−57.2	525.26	1,956.41

*Sell Xerox, hold cash at 5% per annum.

**Buy Xerox again.

EXHIBIT 5-2c

S&P 500

(All prices and dividends adjusted for stock splits and distributions)

Year	Year End Price	Annual Dividend	Annual Percentage Return	Buy & Hold Cumulative Value Index	Market Timing Cumulative Value Index
1962	$ 63.10			100.00	100.00
1963	75.02	2.28	22.5	122.50	122.50
1964	84.75	2.80	16.7	142.95	142.95
1965	92.43	2.72	12.3	160.53	160.53*
1966	86.33	2.87	−3.5	154.91	168.56**
1967	96.47	2.92	15.1	178.30	194.01
1968	103.90	3.07	10.9	197.73	215.16*
1969	92.06	3.16	−8.4	181.12	225.92
1970	92.15	3.14	3.5	187.46	237.22**
1971	102.09	3.07	14.1	213.89	270.67
1972	118.05	3.15	18.7	253.88	321.29*
1973	97.55	3.38	−14.5	217.07	337.35
1974	68.56	3.60	−26.0	160.57	354.22

*Sell S&P 500, hold cash at 5% per annum.

**Buy S&P 500 again.

near. Are there dependable signs of a coming market turning point that can lead investors to the correct decisions? And, if such signs are available, why don't investors take advantage of them?

In pinpointing major market turning points, several factors are helpful, but most important is the outlook for the economy. "Boom and bust" has been a key element of our economic history since the Mayflower. Recessions and economic expansions are continuing to affect everything from politics to the price of eggs. Some of the booms have ended in depressions with very severe effects on the lives of individuals, the most recent being the Depression of the 1930s.

Economic declines have been considerably shorter and less severe since World War II. The Economic Stabilization Act of 1946 committed the federal government to actively combating unemployment, and full employment became a national objective of high priority. This commitment has been combined with growing economist sophistication regarding what must be done to maintain economic growth and avoid depressions. In the process, the old concept of business cycles has largely disappeared from economic language. To many economists, we no longer have depressions, and most recessions are labeled "growth recessions," conveying the impression of a minor interruption in a long-term uptrend. The emphasis today is more on the unpleasant consequences of uninterrupted economic growth, such as environmental pollution, the limited supply of natural resources, and inflation. Even the Department of Commerce's major monthly publication has changed its name from *Business Cycle Developments* to *Business Conditions Digest,* the final bureaucratic step to eradicate the last thoughts of business cycles and economic depressions from our minds.

THE BUSINESS CYCLE AND THE STOCK MARKET

While abandoning the concept of business cycles may be fine for economists, politicians, and the Department of Commerce, it is *not* recommended for investors. The stock market does not seem at all certain that depressions should be relegated to antiquity. It continues to have an unhappy habit of declining in anticipation of economic downturns. Alternatively, the market tends to bottom and begin to advance right in the middle of economic recessions, just when economic news is the worst.

The phenomenon can be seen in Exhibit 5-3, which relates the stock market as measured by the S&P 500 index to economic advances and declines. The shaded areas are periods of significant economic downturn. Notice that the market usually hits its low and starts to advance in the midst of an economic recession and continues to advance until about a year or so prior to the next recession. Then the market usually drops sharply until, in the midst of the new recession, it begins the next advance in anticipation of the coming economic upturn.

The 1962 decline is a major exception since no economic downturn was involved, though there was considerable concern over the possibility of a recession at that time. The 1962 decline followed a period of rampant speculation in the market and included the famous confrontation between President Kennedy and the steel industry. More on the causes of the 1962 decline later.

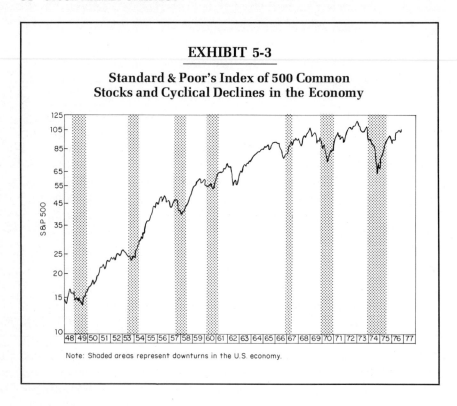

EXHIBIT 5-3

Standard & Poor's Index of 500 Common Stocks and Cyclical Declines in the Economy

Note: Shaded areas represent downturns in the U.S. economy.

The apparent reason for the market's behavior prior to economic downturns is investors' concern that the downturn may become a real depression. The typical pattern goes something like this: As a recession ends, the economy starts to grow, and the growth feeds on itself. Prosperity in one sector of the economy leads to prosperity in another and then another. Usually, demand for new housing is one of the early sectors to resurge. Housing demand results in demand for building materials and appliances and home furnishings. These in turn provide more jobs, and higher employment means more income, which, in turn, leads to more demand for products and services. More demand means more expenditures, more income, and still more demand.

Eventually, demand picks up to such a pace that production cannot keep up. Demand exceeds production, and production cannot be expanded fast enough. Shortages abound. The shortages feed on themselves as consumers and businesses order ahead just to stay even. This excess demand puts pressure on prices, and inflation accelerates. The result is an overheated, inflation-ridden economy that is too successful for its own good.

About this time, inflation becomes a serious political concern. Consequently, government policy begins to lean against the wind, to try to slow down the overheated economy. The objective is to slow the growth in the economy until productive capacity can catch up with demand. Those in government responsible for fiscal policy start talking about a tax increase to reduce excess demand and diminish inflation. The Federal Reserve Board does its part by tightening up on the money supply. Tighter money means higher interest rates, which make housing, capital expenditures, and inventory accumulation more expensive. Again, the objective is to reduce demand and allow capacity to come into balance.

Of course, equilibrium between supply and demand is one of those theoretical niceties that seldom work out in practice. The reason equilibrium does not hold in this situation is the inventory part of the business cycle. Somewhere in here, when the economy is overheated and consumers and business are ordering ahead and maintaining excess inventories in anticipation of continuing high demand, someone pulls the plug and stops buying. It may be a retail firm that suddenly realizes it already has too much inventory. It may be manufacturer who can no longer finance inventories because of high interest rates, or simply the inability to borrow. In any case, someone stops buying and decides to live off his inventories for a while. In turn, his suppliers experience a slowdown in their sales and suddenly get worried about their excess inventories. So they stop ordering, selling off their inventories. And so forth.

The inventory cycle causes a chain reaction. Businesses throughout the economy experience slowing sales. Since their inventories are high, they cut back on production. Unemployment rises rapidly, in turn cutting into consumers' incomes and spending. A recession is the inevitable result.

The worst aspect of this inventory sell-off is that it occurs just when the economy is most vulnerable from a financial viewpoint. As the economy was heating up, consumers and businesses borrowed heavily to finance purchases and inventories. Much of their buying was at high prices, prices which they themselves helped force to excesses by purchases intended to buy before prices went even higher. However, as demand slackens and inventories are sold, commodity prices drop precipitously. Suddenly, businesses find themselves with high cost inventories financed on credit. With sales and profits dropping, they must dump their inventories at cut prices, taking huge losses. Inventories must be sold for amounts insufficient to repay the bank loans financing the inventories. If the firm does not have the cash to make up the losses, bankruptcy is the only alternative. In short, a booming economy necessitates borrowing, which may be disastrous when a recession hits unexpectedly.

This rather oversimplified description of a business downturn also has the mechanism to account for the next upturn. There are naturally correcting forces in the economy. Consumers may delay their purchases of large items, but they keep buying the necessities—food, toothpaste, and so forth. Even delaying purchases of large items, such as cars or appliances, means that sales continue at a reduced level. Eventually retailers, wholesalers, and manufacturers reduce their inventories to reasonable levels and begin to buy again, if at a reduced pace from the economic peak. The inventory cycle runs its course, and the economy naturally stabilizes and begins to expand again.

In recent years, particularly since World War II, national economic policy has been used to combat recessions just as it has tried to slow down a booming economy. Thus, easier money and expanded government expenditures tend to buoy up the economy and help it recover from a recession. The problem is inflation. As inflation has accelerated in recent years, the federal government has been reluctant to move as rapidly and as strongly to offset recessions. Early in the recession, the inflation rate may be very high as a residual effect of the economic boom. Federal actions to halt the economic decline would adversely contribute to the inflation rate. Consequently, federal policy has more and more tended to tough it out further into a recession than previously, allowing a higher level of unemployment in hopes of *winning* the inflation battle. Political leaders have been more willing than before to accept the political risks of high unemployment rather than face the risks of high inflation.

Unfortunately, there are high financial risks in this strategy. A longer recession means a more severe inventory cycle and greater risk of major bankruptcies. As we have discussed, the excessive borrowing required in the economic boom to finance inventories at inflated prices can cause severe stress in a recession. It increases the risk of the inventory sell-off getting out of hand. As business slows, more and more firms dump inventories, and more dumping means lower commodity prices. If prices drop low enough, a firm may not be able to meet its bank loans and other payables. These payables are other firms' receivables. A bankruptcy at one firm can cascade into another bankruptcy and, like dominos, right through the economy, causing mayhem. Since inflation precludes government action to offset this phenomenon, the risks of a serious economic problem are apparent.

Recessions are a natural and even necessary part of the economic system. While recessions inevitably cause severe hardships for many individuals, they do have positive effects—eliminating inefficient firms, for example. But, on the whole, no one wins in a recession, and the stock market is justifiably concerned. Thus, the market peaks and starts to descend at the first hint of a recession on the horizon. Similarly, the market usually hits bottom just when the economic news is worst, when the dangers of a recession collapsing into a full-scale depression are the greatest. Somewhere in the midst of this, the stock market sees the light at the end of the tunnel, sees that the recession is going to end and that economic recovery will follow. Then, it starts to rally, often a very strong rally, before the recession ends. While the economy is still mired in the recession, the market sees the coming business upturn, sees that this time a major depression will be averted, and responds accordingly.

PREDICTING THE BUSINESS CYCLE

This is a rather oversimplified view of the developments in the stock market surrounding an economic downturn. But the process is remarkably consistent, having recurred regularly since World War II (as shown in Exhibit 5-3) and countless times before that. This means investors must make every effort to predict the next recession—or the next business upturn—as early as possible. By the time the recession hits, the market may already be down substantially. What techniques are available to predict business upturns and downturns?

The United States Department of Commerce has for years published a set of Leading Indicators of the economy. These are a composite of several individual factors, all of which have historically led turning points in the economy. Among the indices considered are housing permits, real money balances, the length of factory workweeks, the layoff rate in manufacturing, the number of new business formations, changes in sensitive materials prices, and, of all things, stock prices.

Exhibit 5-4 shows the Department of Commerce Leading Indicator series as well as stock prices (S&P 500) and economic downturns (shaded areas). The Leading Indicators do tend to lead the economy. In general, they show deterioration in the economy before a recession begins and they start to turn up just before the recession ends. This

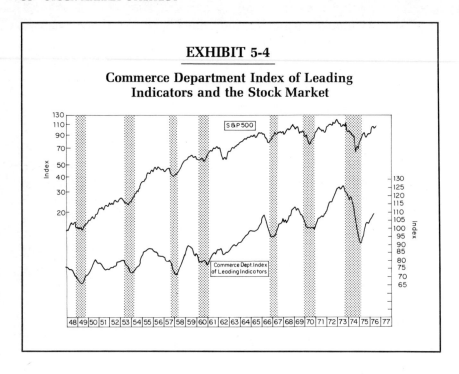

EXHIBIT 5-4

**Commerce Department Index of Leading
Indicators and the Stock Market**

weakening and strengthening of the Leading Indicators is indeed indicative of forthcoming trends in the overall economy.

However, note that stock prices are included in the Leading Indicators of the economy. In fact, stock prices, as we have already discussed, are one of the better series used in these Leading Indicators. Thus, it is difficult to use the Leading Indicators of the economy to predict the stock market. This is especially true if two serious mechanical problems are considered. First, there is usually a delay of about two months in publishing the Leading Indicators. It takes time to gather, process, and verify all the necessary data. If one is trying to use Exhibit 5-4 in a live situation for investment decision making, this delay must be considered.

Additionally, one cannot determine that the Leading Indicators have peaked or bottomed until subsequent months are reported showing that the series have changed direction. Suppose April is the low month. One does not become aware of this until May and June are reported showing an upturn. Then, there is the reporting delay to consider, so one does not learn the June number until, say, August. In August, we learn that April was the low. But, by this time, the stock market will likely have moved substantially. Thus, the Department of Commerce Leading Indicators can at best provide a clue as to the future market directions and certainly must be used in conjunction with other information.

CORPORATE PROFITS

The profits of business corporations are obviously closely correlated with the business cycle. When the economy is advancing and corporations are prospering, profits are likely to be growing smartly. On the other hand, in economic downturns, corporate profits are adversely affected. In a severe recession, profits can drop precipitously.

As a reflection of the health of the economy, corporate profits provide additional clues to coming peaks and troughs in both the business cycle and stock prices. Typically, the danger signals are that the economy is doing so well that things cannot possibly improve. Corporate profits are soaring and unemployment is dropping so rapidly that the improvement cannot continue. Exhibit 5-5 shows the relationship

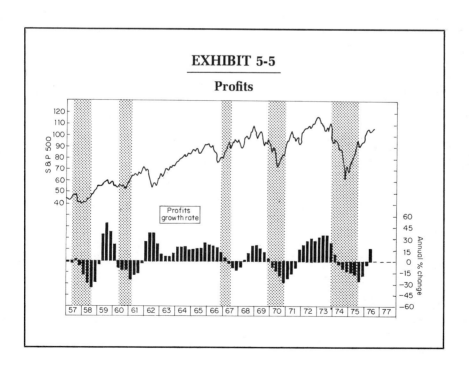

EXHIBIT 5-5

Profits

between the rate of gain in corporate profits and the stock market as measured by the S&P 500. The chart shows the annual gain in durable goods profits, an especially sensitive category, but almost any aggregate profit series will display the same phenomenon. The market has a tendency to peak about the time that the rate of gain in profits is at its maximum, when corporate success is at its highest. Conversely, when profits growth is at its worst, when the decline is in full swing, is the time to be optimistic on the stock market.

Unfortunately, leads and lags between the stock market and profits are not consistent. Sometimes the market anticipates the economic outlook further into the future than other times. Each cycle can be different, but the same principle holds—sell on the good news and buy on the bad. If the economy is booming and the market is reaching new highs, watch for the "this time things are different" story. It always appears at market peaks, and always explains why *this time* the boom can last forever. Of course, the story merely reflects the temperament of the times, the basic optimism that has caused the market to reach its high level.

The bear story at market bottoms is just the opposite. This time there really could be a depression; the economy isn't going to rebound. This in turn is the reason that the market does bottom. When the "this time is different" story appears to reinforce and extend the current stock market trend, prepare for a shift in market direction.

MONETARY POLICY

The importance of monetary policy for the economy has been widely discussed. Monetary policy is closely tied to the business cycle; indeed it is one of the principal tools used by Washington policy makers to manage the economy. Consequently, monetary policy is important for the stock market.

Exhibit 5-6 is a convenient summary of monetary policy and the stock market. The chart shows specific expansionist and restrictive moves by the Federal Reserve Board. Three categories of policy actions by the Fed are charted: changes in bank discount rates, changes in reserve requirements for banks, and changes in stock market margin requirements. Any move in these three policy areas that can be considered expansive is charted as an upward step. Restrictive actions are charted as downward steps.

In 1968, there was a long sequence of restrictive moves intended to

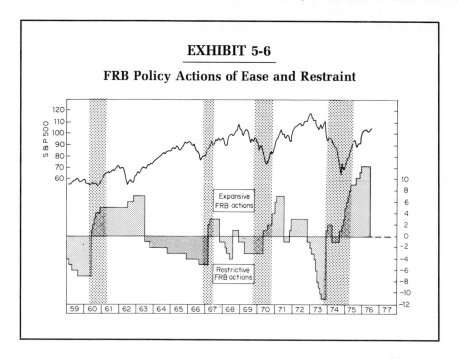

EXHIBIT 5-6

FRB Policy Actions of Ease and Restraint

slow down an overheated, inflationary economy. These restrictive actions ultimately contributed to the market decline of 1969–70. On the other hand, 1970 and 1971 were marked by a series of expansionist moves intended to end the recession and get the economy moving ahead. The effect on the stock market was very favorable, and the market advanced significantly.

1974 was a particularly interesting example of the Federal Reserve and the market. The year began with the Arab oil embargo superimposed on a classic economic boom with an accelerating rate of inflation. The oil shortage and long lines at gasoline stations were rapidly slowing the economic boom. A mini-recession induced by energy shortages had begun. Consequently, the Fed had shifted to an expansive—purists will insist accommodative is a better word—status.

Normally, this would be a positive sign. But, as the oil embargo ended, the economy rebounded and inflation continued to accelerate. Suddenly, the Fed shifted back to a restrictive stance to lean against the economic rebound. This is shown in Exhibit 5-6 by the move on April 24, 1974, raising the bank discount rate. This particular action was indicative of a general tightening by the Fed, which resulted in accelerating interest rates. The stock market dropped sharply and the 1973–1974 bear market became one of the worst since the 1930s.

Then, on September 15, November 13, and December 18, 1974, the Federal Reserve began a series of expansive moves, which continued into 1975. The stock market hit a low in mid-October and the final low as measured by the Dow Jones Industrial Averages was on December 6. The initial expansive moves by the Fed were approximately coincident with the market bottom, illustrating the importance of monetary policy for stock market investors.

The leads and lags between monetary policy and the stock market are not so consistent or so regular that one can predict the market peak or bottom with precision. But there does seem to be ample opportunity to observe the general policies of the Federal Reserve Board and take action. When the market has been declining, the economy is clearly in a downturn, and the Fed starts a series of expansive moves, a buying opportunity is approaching. Alternatively, when the stock market and the economy are booming and the Fed is increasing margin requirements, ordering higher bank reserves, and raising the rediscount rate, a market peak is approaching.

INTEREST RATES

Interest rates, particularly shorter-term interest rates, reflect both the business cycle and monetary policy. Interest rates on U.S. Treasury bills, commercial paper, and federal funds—the rates at which banks lend reserves to one another—are particularly sensitive to the interaction of monetary policy and economic activity. The basic pattern is for short-term interest rates to advance slowly as the economy advances. As the economy begins to overheat and nears the peak in business activity, short-term interest rates reach high levels. This reflects both demand for cash resulting from business activity and tightening monetary policy as the Fed leans against the wind to try to cool the economy and slow inflation. Interest rates may remain high until well into the recession because of these two factors.

Later, however, as the economy slows and the recession solidly takes hold, short-term interest rates drop very rapidly. While lessening economic activity means lower demand for cash, the more important phenomenon is the Fed's easing of monetary policy. This easing injects money into the economic system to stave off a depression and get the economy moving on an upward course again. Exhibit 5-7 shows short-

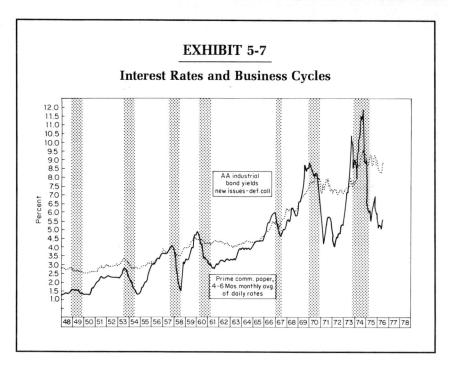

EXHIBIT 5-7

Interest Rates and Business Cycles

term interest rates in relation to business cycles. Note the behavior of short rates as a recession approaches, and near the end of the recession.

Short-term interest rates are especially important to stock market investors at both these times. The tight money and rising interest rates associated with an economic boom are indicative of a coming peak in economic activity. Tight money and high short-term interest rates are designed to slow the economy. This policy inevitably succeeds. Since rising rates are a forecaster of a coming business cycle peak, they are useful information for investors because, as we already know, the market is likely to peak well before the business cycle peak.

Equally important is the fact that short rates offer a very attractive alternative to investors just when the stock market is losing momentum. As the stock market approaches its peak, investors analyzing the risk/reward aspects of the market begin to see only marginal room for advancement in prices and the risk of a very large drop—in short, a very dubious risk/reward opportunity. On the other hand, Treasury bills and high-grade commercial paper, both virtually riskless, are offering high rates of return. The incentive to switch funds out of the market and into these short-term money-market instruments becomes overwhelming.

At the market bottom in the midst of a recession, the opposite is the case. Stock prices have been battered down to low levels, providing very large potential on the upside. Short-term interest rates, on the other hand, are probably plummeting rapidly. Often the rates drop 50 percent or so. Declining short-term interest rates are indicative both of a recovering economy—rather, about to recover—and a switch in the risk/reward ratio in favor of stocks.

Another important factor is value; traditionally, stock market analysts have used price/earnings ratios as a helpful measure of value. Everyone recognizes that P/Es are a bit crude. For one thing, you are never really sure what future earnings will be. Differences in accounting are another problem. But P/Es are handy, easy to understand, and about the best available measure of value.

Exhibit 5-8 shows the P/E of the S&P index of 425[1] industrial stocks since 1959. The chart uses current price divided by earnings in the

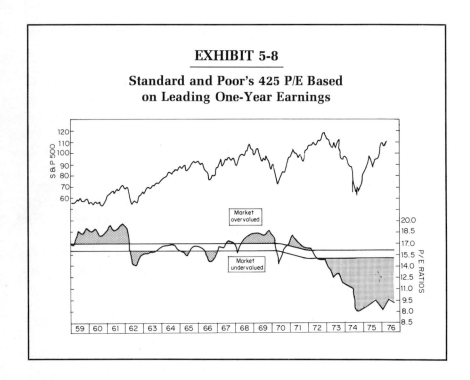

EXHIBIT 5-8

**Standard and Poor's 425 P/E Based
on Leading One-Year Earnings**

[1]The S&P 425 became the S&P 400 on July 1, 1976.

coming year, so it depends to an extent on one's ability to forecast earnings. In spite of this, it seems that over the past 15 years, a normal range for the P/E of the S&P 425 might be 15 to 17. When the market P/E has gotten much above this level—for example, in 1962—the market has been vulnerable to a decline. On the other hand, when the P/E of the market index has dropped below 15, the market has been approaching a buying opportunity.

Again, unusually high or low P/Es do not mean that a market turning point is imminent, only that it is approaching. The market can stay overvalued or undervalued for long periods of time, often a year or more. The market maintained an unusually high P/E from 1959 to 1962. It can also stay undervalued for long periods. An old Wall Street adage is that stocks look terribly cheap a long time before the market bottoms.

The market drop in 1962 was an example of an overvalued market that collapsed because prices got out of line with value. The economic outlook and monetary policy factors apparently had little to do with it. The market rally was sparked by economic optimism generated by the Kennedy administration's intention to "get the country moving again." The rally was led by a boom in electronics stocks in response to the space race and plans to put a man on the moon in the decade of the sixties. There was great public anguish about our national status in science versus the Soviet Union, a sharp jump in attendance at science courses in high schools and colleges, and a rush to buy any new stock with a scientific-sounding name. Any new issue with a name ending in "-ics" or better still "-ionics" was virtually assured of a rapid rise in price.

By late 1961, stock prices far exceeded any reasonable estimate of value, buying interest dried up, and stock prices took a sharp drop, even though the economy was still growing. Corporate earnings growth did slow, but profits kept advancing. There was no economic downturn until 1966. The major explanation for the 1962 market peak is a speculative binge that finally pushed prices into the overvalued range. When the speculative binge ran out of gas, prices tumbled. It was fun and profitable while it lasted, but, like Camelot, it didn't last forever.

KEY MARKET PARTICIPANTS

In addition to the economic outlook, the course of monetary policy, and the value available in the stock market, the attitudes of key market participants need to be evaluated. These participants are interesting because some of them are consistently right on the future course of the market. Others, however, are consistently wrong. As long as they are consistent, we can benefit from their counsel.

Large corporate shareholders are of particular interest because of their excellent track record. This is not surprising because they should be more aware of the prospects for their company and its intrinsic value. When there is a large number of corporate secondaries (public sales of stock by large shareholders, registered with the Securities and Exchange Commission, which take place under conditions of full disclosure of corporate financial records) one can be sure that these stockholders feel that current market prices fully reflect the value of their company. On the other hand, when there are few secondaries, one reason is that large shareholders feel their stock is undervalued in the market and are unwilling to sell.

This phenomenon is shown in Exhibit 5-9. Note the large number of secondaries in 1968 and 1972. On the other hand, there were relatively few in 1970, 1966, and so on. The chart shows the number of secondaries, not the dollar value of the secondaries. It reflects the decisions of a large number of companies and their large shareholders and is not unduly influenced by a single giant offering.

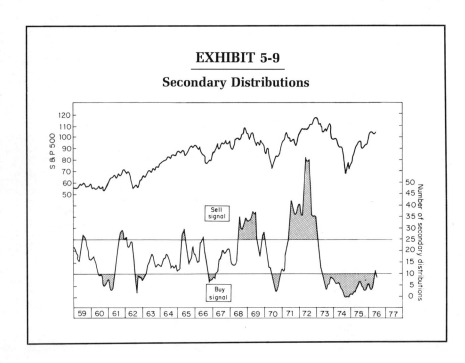

EXHIBIT 5-9

Secondary Distributions

Odd-lotters form another group of market participants. Whenever they are heavy short-sellers relative to total selling activity, it indicates that they are unusually pessimistic. And since odd-lot short sellers are usually wrong, it often means that a market bottom is very near. This occurred in 1962, 1966, and again in 1970, as shown in Exhibit 5-10.

Institutional investors are fond of proclaiming that this unfortunate predilection on the part of odd-lotters simply reflects their lack of sophistication. Small investors just don't have a chance, so the reasoning goes, against the large institutions with their Wall Street information sources, high-powered security analysts, computers, and time-tested portfolio managers. Maybe so, but the data on mutual funds, until recently the only investment institutions required to report their transactions on a regular basis, do not support the allegation. It seems that mutual funds in the aggregate, not any particular mutual fund, have the same tendency to take the wrong stance at market turning points.

Exhibit 5-11 shows the aggregate cash reserves of mutual funds along with the S&P 500 stock index. Note that mutual funds have a tendency to hold large cash reserves at market bottoms—just when they should be fully invested. Conversely, they are fully invested at market peaks,

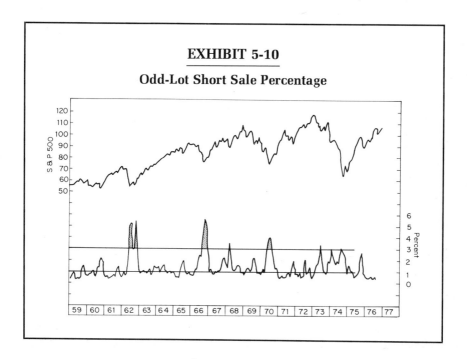

EXHIBIT 5-10

Odd-Lot Short Sale Percentage

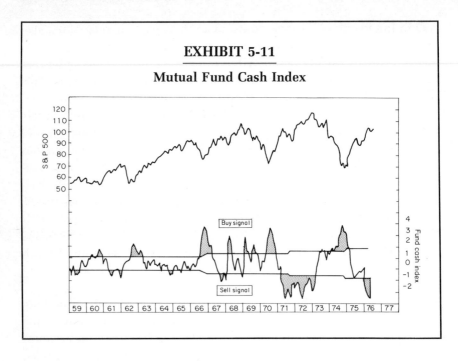

EXHIBIT 5-11

Mutual Fund Cash Index

when they should have high cash reserves. The last time mutual funds were fully invested was in April 1972. While the stock market averages were advancing during this period, the majority of stocks were peaking and beginning to decline.

TECHNICAL FACTORS

As we have seen, the stock market is often very farsighted in its predictions. It often knows about recessions long before the Leading Indicators and the leading economists. It is equally skillful at forecasting business upturns. In short, the stock market has a forecasting record that few professional prognosticators can equal. The stock market is such a sensitive barometer of so many factors—economic, psychological, political, financial, and so forth—that it reflects the wisdom and emotions of millions of investors. It is the accumulated information, pressures, and guesses of an extremely broad segment of the world's population.

Many analysts believe that investors can greatly benefit from studying the actions of the market and trying to determine what they mean.

What is the market telling us now? Does the market know something we do not know? Suppose all the experts are telling us one thing—and the stock market starts moving in the other direction. Could the experts be wrong? Does the market know something they do not? Studying the behavior of the stock market in conjunction with what we already know about recessions, interest rates, monetary policy, and value can be very helpful. Like anything else, it is dangerous to place sole reliance on stock market technical factors. Nevertheless, they have a useful role.

One of the basic tenets of technical analysis is that stock market advances take longer to develop than market declines. The market tends to move up for much longer periods than it declines. As a result, market tops are much more diffuse, often taking months to unfold as the market fluctuates in a high trading range before dropping relatively quickly.

As a market gradually approaches its cyclical peak, the rate of advance slows dramatically, giving the astute investor considerable time to realize what is happening—that the bull market is running out of steam—and plenty of time to sell. Even if he sells early, he probably is not missing much of the total advance, while the greedy investor who hangs on for the last flurry before the bear market is taking a high-risk gamble for a relatively small return.

The tendency for the market to slow its rate of advance as the bull market cycle matures can be seen in Exhibit 5-12. Here, past bull markets have been divided into four equal time segments. If a particular market advance lasted 40 months, Exhibit 5-12 shows the portion of the overall gain that occurred in the first 10 months, the second 10 months, and so on. On average, over the last seven bull markets, 42 percent of the overall gain has occurred in the first quarter, 64 percent by the halfway mark, and 81 percent by the three-quarter mark. The last quarter of the market advance provided only 19 percent of the overall gain. The investor who sells early is probably not missing much, and is avoiding a major risk of holding through the coming market decline.

One must also consider that the principal haven for stock market funds during bear markets is short-term securities such as commercial paper, Treasury bills, and certificates of deposit. The rates of return on these instruments are usually rising toward attractive levels just at the time that the investor should become concerned over the market outlook. In short, the principal alternatives are beginning to provide the most favorable rates of return just as stocks are losing their attractiveness. This is further inducement to sell early.

EXHIBIT 5-12

S&P 500 and Market Momentum

Bull Market Dates Bottom – Peak	Duration, months	Percentage Rise in Each Time Quartile
		1 2 3 4
6/49 – 1/53	43	40 + 28 + 17 + 15 = 100%
9/53 – 8/56	35	25 + 30 + 33 + 12 = 100%
10/57 – 8/59	22	21 + 30 + 30 + 19 = 100%
10/60 – 12/61	14	49 + 25 + 5 + 21 = 100%
6/62 – 2/66	44	44 + 23 + 17 + 16 = 100%
10/66 – 11/68	25	61 + 8 + 4 + 27 = 100%
5/70 – 1/73	32	53 + 11 + 14 + 22 = 100%
AVERAGE	31	42 + 22 + 17 + 19 = 100%

THE ADVANCE/DECLINE INDEX

The majority of individual stocks usually turn down before the peak in the market averages. Investors seem to lose confidence in the majority of stocks long before they lose confidence in the giant companies that dominate the stock market averages. As bull markets near their end, investor attention is focused on a small stable of superstar stocks which require more and more inflowing cash to maintain their upside momentum. Consequently, the average investor will see his stocks start to decline before the stock market indices. This is further incentive to sell early.

Interest rates are another reason many stocks peak before the averages. Rising interest rates first put pressure on stocks that are held primarily for yield, such as utilities, autos, oils, steels, and other mature industries selling at relatively low P/Es. Less impact is expected on high P/E glamour stocks, since no one buys such stocks for yield. As competition between short-term yields and dividends on securities intensifies, disintermediation puts pressure on the stock market, first through yield vehicles, but later throughout the list.

The tendency for many stocks to peak prior to the peak in the popular averages can be illustrated by an Advance/Decline Index. An Advance/Decline Index is simply the cumulative total of the number of stocks advancing on a given day less the number of stocks declining. Pick an arbitrary starting point, say 1,000. Suppose on the first day, 750 stocks are up and 700 are down. (Ignore stocks unchanged for the day.) For the first day, 750 up less 700 down nets out to +50. So the Advance/ Decline Index becomes 1,000 + 50 = 1,050. On the second day, 725 are up and 750 are down. (Again, ignore stocks unchanged.) The result for the day is 725 − 750 or a net of −25. The Advance/Decline Index then becomes 1,050 − 25 = 1,025.

As a market peak approaches, the very large companies that dominate the popular market averages (Dow Jones Industrials, S&P 500, New York Stock Exchange Composite) keep rising so the averages are rising. But the majority of stocks are actually declining. The Advance/Decline Index, which gives equal weight to each stock, large or small, is also dropping. In the extreme case, consider what would happen if the 30 stocks in the Dow Jones Industrial Average were up but all the other 1,500 or so stocks on the New York Stock Exchange were down. The Dow Jones Industrial Average would be up, an apparent sign of market strength. But the Advance/Decline Index would drop by −1,470 (30 advances minus 1,500 declines), exhibiting extreme market weakness.

Exhibit 5-13 shows an Advance/Decline Index for several market cycles. For the market peaks, recent experience is that the Advance/ Decline Index peaked earlier than the market, that is, at the peak in

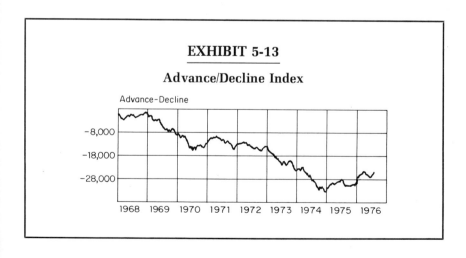

EXHIBIT 5-13

Advance/Decline Index

Advance-Decline

the averages, the Advance/Decline Index was below its previous high. In the jargon of technical analysts, this is nonconfirmation by the Advance/Decline Index. Both the Averages and the Advance/Decline Index simultaneously making new highs would be a confirmation of continued market strength. The "nonconfirmation" is considered very weak.

UPTRENDS AND DOWNTRENDS

Finally, there is one last technical observation that must be made. It is such a simple concept that it is impossible to state without sounding trite, but here it is. The market starts an advance by going *up;* conversely, it starts a decline by going *down.* To illustrate, suppose the economy is deep in a recession and the market has already dropped a long way from its peak. Suppose stocks look undervalued and the President of the United States goes on television saying the economic outlook is better than most people think and, if he had any money, he would be buying stocks. Suppose interest rates have started to decline and the Fed had made an expansive move or two. But the stock market is still dropping like a stone. Question: Has the new bull market begun? *No!* Stocks are still declining. The bull market doesn't begin until stocks start advancing. The bull market may be close to beginning. The right conditions are developing. True, if you buy early, you may turn out to be a hero and get prices very close to the ultimate lows. But it is safer to wait until the market itself is telling you it's ready to go up. And the way it tells you is by starting to advance. Admittedly, it sounds trite. But it can save you a lot of money.

How does one tell that the market has really started to advance or decline? How does one distinguish a new trend from a rally in a bear market? There is no foolproof method. If there were, the stock market problem would be solved. All the risk would be removed and everyone would win. Probably the best approach is to compare the current market highs with the last, or the current lows with the previous lows. Suppose we are looking for a market bottom. In late 1974, conditions were developing to suggest a market bottom might be close. The economy was in a severe recession. Stock prices had dropped nearly 50 percent from their highs in early 1973. The Fed was making expansive moves and short-term interest rates were dropping. Mutual funds were raising cash and odd-lot short selling was increasing. There were virtually no secondary stock offerings.

But stock prices had not started to move up. On October 3, the S&P 500 average hit a low for the cycle of 62.28. Then stock prices rallied into November, only to decline again in December. However, on December 6, the S&P 500 average halted its decline at 65.01, above the earlier low. From there, stock prices moved up sharply, and another cyclical market advance had begun.

The clue was that the December low was above the October low. The market weakness in December was not as pronounced as the market weakness in October. The market was gathering strength from its very battered state.

Admittedly, a higher low (or, at a peak, a lower high) in the market seems like skimpy evidence on which to base an important investment judgment. Taken alone, it certainly would be. But for astute investors aware of the environment required to get a bull market started, it turned out to be an important clue.

SUMMING UP

There remain, of course, a number of important stock market factors which cannot be quantified or predicted. Wars, political events, and the health of the President of the United States are in this category. The market dropped sharply on news of President Eisenhower's heart attacks and the assassination of President Kennedy. The market rallied for several months after President Johnson announced that he would not run for reelection. By and large, however, these events had only a transitory effect on the market, whatever their personal and political implications.

None of this is intended to suggest that it is possible to forecast accurately what the stock market will do in the next month or even year. But there is considerable evidence that one can discern periods when the stock market is approaching significant turning points. On the sell side, when

- the market has been advancing for a period of time, and the economy is booming

- corporate profits are accelerating and unemployment is low

- volume on the stock exchange is high and stock market successes are prominent in the news

- new secondary offerings are frequent and mutual funds are fully invested and bragging about their recent performance successes

- the Fed is tightening and interest rates are rising

think about getting out of the market. Your commitment to sell should be reinforced if market commentators are straining to explain that this is really only the beginning, that things are about to become even better because the national economy is no longer susceptible to those annoying old recessions. When these events take place, the market is getting near a peak. It may be in a week or a month or it may be several months away. No one knows how far speculation will run this time around. Sometimes it's robust, and sometimes it dies quickly. But the astute investor will want to become very wary and begin to move out of the stock market. No one can tell you when to make this move or just how. That's a matter for judgment and guesswork, but the direction to go is very clear.

On the buy side, when

- the market is down and business is in a cyclical downturn— whether it's called a recession or not

- Wall Street experts are pessimistic and people are worrying about a depression

- the Federal Reserve has adopted an expansive stance to get the economy moving and short-term interest rates are dropping

- mutual funds have built up substantial cash reserves, indicating the pessimism of major institutional investors

begin to think about getting back into the market. No one can tell you which day to buy. You can wait for that big build-up in odd-lot short selling, if you wish, but even that signal can be off by months. In the end you are left to your own judgment to decide when the coming business upturn is barely visible on the horizon. You must make this judgment in full recognition that you will probably miss the real bottom. But, whatever you decide, buying anywhere close to the bottom certainly beats buying at the top.

CHECKLIST

As we have noted, it is impossible to predict what the stock market is likely to do over the next day or week or month or even year. In short periods, the random walk concept is just too powerful. A few people are lucky enough to make accurate short-term forecasts for a time, but eventually they all stumble. Rather, we have attempted to focus attention on the longer market cycle suggesting that every couple of years or so a basic decision must be made. Is it a time to buy, or a time to sell? There are a number of helpful guidelines in making these decisions. We have reviewed some of these. But you must apply your own judgment, knowledge, and insight and make your own market forecast.

Two checklists are provided—the *Time to Buy* and the *Time to Sell* checklists. With a little homework and digging for information, all of which is readily available in the financial press, almost anyone should be able to complete the checklist. Remember, the answers change continually, so the checklists must be kept current. With the information in hand, you should be in a good position to make the necessary judgments. Keep in mind that this is not intended to be a system to beat the market. In truth, there is no such system. Rather, we have attempted to pinpoint the factors that investment theory and experience indicate are pertinent.

Most frequently you will not get 100 percent on either the Buy or Sell checklist. For one reason, you are most likely to be in between the best times to buy—they usually occur about once every four years or so. Consequently, you usually must decide whether a bull market is in progress and if it has sufficient longevity to make participation worthwhile.

If you have established your investment objectives correctly as described in Chapter Four, this decision on the market outlook is extremely important and worth much of your time and attention. Make the market outlook decision correctly, or anywhere near correctly, and you will go a very long way toward achieving investment success.

The Time to Buy Checklist

Business Cycle

1. Is business activity nationally in a downtrend? Do you foresee the end of this downtrend?

2. Is inflation decelerating?

3. Are the Leading Indicators starting to advance?

4. Are corporate profits declining, and do you expect them to begin advancing soon?

5. Are inventories declining?

6. Are most economic forecasts—from nonpolitical sources—very pessimistic? Is the economic news largely negative?

Monetary Policy/Interest Rates

1. Has the Federal Reserve Board begun to make expansive moves—lowering the bank discount rate, decreasing reserve requirements, lowering stock market margin requirements?

2. Is the chairman of the Fed expressing more concern about unemployment and economic growth than about inflation and an overheated economy?

3. Are short-term interest rates (Treasury bills, commercial paper, federal funds) declining? Have they declined enough for the economy to start expanding? (Typically, short rates drop 50 percent or so during a recession.)

Value

1. What is the P/E of the market? Is it approaching or below the market P/E at the last cyclical low in the market?

Market Participants

1. Are few large corporate shareholders making secondary offerings? Has the new issue market virtually dried up?

2. Are odd-lotters shorting heavily?

3. Are mutual funds heavily in cash?

Technical

1. Has the market been declining for some months from the previous cyclical peak? (The median twentieth century bear market has lasted 18 to 22 months.)

2. Has the market declined a significant percentage from the previous cyclical high? (The median twentieth century bear market decline is 41 percent.)

3. Has the market accelerated its rate of decline? (The last stages of bear markets tend to show the steepest rates of decline.)

4. Has the market bottomed and started to advance? Did the last dip in the market fail to take the popular indices as low as the previous dip?

Personal

1. If you have been invested, have you lost a lot of money in the market recently?

2. Are your friends, relatives, business associates urging you to avoid the stock market? Or, have they all totally lost interest in the subject?

3. Is the market risk of your *current* portfolio (See Chapter Four) lower than you originally thought it should be?

Summary

If the answer to all or many of these questions is "Yes," there is an excellent chance that this is a time to buy.

The Time to Sell Checklist

Business Cycle

1. Is there growing evidence of a business cycle peak?

2. Is inflation accelerating?

3. Are the Leading Indicators declining?

4. Has the rate of gain of corporate profits slowed, or is the current high rate of gain too good to last?

5. Are inventories rising?

6. Are most economic forecasts you see optimistic?

Monetary Policy/Interest Rates

1. Has the Federal Reserve Board begun to make tightening moves—raising the bank discount rate, increasing bank reserve requirements, raising stock market margin requirements?

2. Is the chairman of the Fed talking more about inflation and an overheated economy than about unemployment and economic growth?

3. Are short-term interest rates (Treasury bills, commercial paper, federal funds) rising? How high are they? (Typically, short rates double during a business expansion.)

Value

1. What is the P/E of the market? Is it approaching or above the market P/E at the last cyclical peak in the market?

Market Participants

1. Are large corporate shareholders offering secondaries? Are new stock issues described frequently in the financial areas?

2. Are odd-lotters doing relatively little short selling?

3. Are mutual funds fully committed to stocks? Are their cash positions low?

Technical

1. Has the market been advancing for many months from the previous cyclical low? (The median twentieth century bull market advance has been 26 months.)

2. Has the market advanced a hefty percentage from the previous cyclical low? (The median twentieth century advance is 90 percent.)

3. Has the market slowed its rate of advance? (Only 19 percent of the advance typically occurs in the last time quarter.)

4. Is market breadth deteriorating; are relatively few stocks advancing? Is the Advance/Decline Index underperforming the popular averages?

5. Has the market peaked? Did the last rally fail to reach the previous high in this cycle?

Personal

1. Have you made a lot of money recently in the market?

2. Are your friends, relatives, business associates urging you to invest more so you can make easy profits like they have?

3. Is the market risk of your current portfolio (see Chapter Four) higher than you originally thought it should be?

Summary

If the answers to all or many of these questions is "Yes," there is an excellent chance that, for you, it is a time to sell.

WHY SO FEW TELL TIME CORRECTLY

If market tops and bottoms are indeed detectable in at least a general way, why don't more people act on them? There are a number of reasons, and not all of them reflect favorably on human nature.

For one thing, when it comes right down to it, most of us don't have the fortitude or insight or courage to do the right thing, even in the face of strong evidence, if it means going against the crowd and acting contrary to popular investment trends.

In addition, this reluctance to make the correct decisions as opposed to the popular decisions, to sell when others are buying and buy when others are selling, is reinforced by the system under which institutions manage investments. Some of the influences are:

Size

Some portfolios are so huge relative to trading volume that their managers regard selling and rebuying as too costly, too cumbersome.

Managers of these giant portfolios may find it easier to lean toward a stock-selection strategy geared to long-term returns. The buy-and-hold policy has worked well for years. Patience has its rewards, so why not weather the declines and stay in for even more gain in the advances? Selling and then rebuying involves two big decisions. To be wrong on either, is to miss significant gains. In short, doing nothing means at least keeping up with the market.

Vested Interests

Brokerage houses and other investment institutions are subject to this influence. Since stockbrokers earn their income from commissions, they depend on investors participating in the market. No broker can afford to advise clients to put their money in a savings bank because the market outlook for the next two years is unfavorable. Stock and bond departments of large institutions operate under a similar bias. Since they're separate entities, each has a vested interest in maintaining investments in its particular segment of the financial market. What manager of a common stock department would shift large sums out of stocks and into the bond department? Even if market conditions were to improve, the manager might not get them back. Better to ride out the storm in a fully invested position.

Client Pressures

Clients can also be a very serious problem. Many clients of investment managers are unsophisticated about the stock market. That's why they hired a professional in the first place. When everything is going well in the economy and the stock market is booming, clients rarely listen to the investment manager who thinks it's time to sell. They are having too much fun telling their friends about their market success. How can they sell when everyone else is profiting? Of course, just the opposite happens at market bottoms. When sophisticated investment managers want to begin buying, clients have lost all confidence and want to sell. The advisors have to convince not only themselves but also their clients that it's time to buy. This double handicap may be too much.

Competitive Management

A recent development in the pension area makes going against the trend particularly difficult. Many large pension funds are hiring several money managers to competitively manage their investments. Usually, these investment managers are selected because of their particular success in such investment areas as managing bond portfolios or picking hot stocks. Under this arrangement, several different firms simultaneously handle stock market investments for a particular pension fund. Each handles a segment of the total portfolio, and the one who does the best (often measured over a very short time span, say three or six months) receives additional funds to manage. Additional funds mean higher fees. This competitive environment with very short-term rewards and penalties makes going against the stock market trend particularly difficult.

Suppose some bright investment managers feel that the current market is too speculative, detect a coming peak, and want to sell. They start selling while competitors remain fully invested and are telling the client that fully invested is the only place to be. Since the bright money managers would have to be very lucky to pick the exact market peak, the chances are good that they are starting to sell a little early, while the market is still advancing. Because they are selling and are partially in cash, they start to underperform both the advancing market and the competitors. And all the competitors, no doubt, are telling clients that it is crazy to sell when such great profits can be made. Is this any way to get additional funds to invest? Or is it a good way to lose a valuable client? The end result once again is that it's easier not to sell. Ride it out with everyone else.

A VIEW FROM 1927

Lest anyone be offended by these comments about human nature or, even worse, lest anyone suspect that the author considers himself in any way immune to this problem, consider the reflections of R. W. McNeel in *Beating the Stock Market,* published in 1927, just before the greatest speculative boom which ended in 1929 in the greatest stock market crash.

McNeel attributed investors' failure to sell during speculative binges to weaknesses inherent in human nature. He mentions instinctive fear, the tendency to do as the crowd does, the inability to think for oneself against the overwhelming trend of others. These factors tend to make all men panic together as the market falls in the face of worsening economic news. And we all take comfort in the fact that we are all losing money.

McNeel also mentions egotism, which causes men to think well of their own activities. Thus, we attribute our speculative success in the stock market to our own genius at selecting hot stocks, not to the speculative boom in the overall market, which has made all stocks go up. As a result, our egotism may lead us to increase the margin on our already overly inflated stocks in the sure and certain prediction that our success will continue to lead to even greater gains. Of course, when the speculative boom ends, this overextended position collapses and makes the subsequent decline even more severe.

In short, stock market success depends only in part on knowing when stocks are low and when they are high, when they are cheap and when they are dear. It depends as well on whether investors have sufficient strength of character and sufficient willpower to conquer those instincts and emotions and tendencies inherent in their own natures, which dictate actions contrary to sound speculative policy. If they can develop powers of independent thought, can be ruled in their actions by reason rather than emotion, can keep their heads when others are losing theirs and are following blind and unreasoning instincts, and can, above all, curb that greed and avarice which, far from being satisfied with increased riches, grows and develops with the acquisition of each new dollar, they can make money through speculation in the stock market.

It is a problem in self-mastery and self-discipline as much as one in finance.

SIX

Bargain Hunting

Medicine is one of the most harried professions in our society. Despite the popular image of Wednesdays on the golf course and no house calls ever, medical doctors are interrupted morning, noon, and night by the ringing of telephones. Chances are the call has to do with a medical emergency and must be dealt with immediately.

What is not widely known, however, is that M.D.'s are prime targets of securities salesmen. Since M.D.'s usually have above-average incomes and above-average investable assets, they are prime sales prospects for stocks, bonds, and other investment vehicles. When the doctor's phone rings, it might be a patient with a medical emergency or it might be Merrill Lynch.

Business executives, other professional persons, anyone who, it can be assumed, has money to invest has probably had similar experiences. The phone rings, you answer, and on the other end of the line is someone trying to sell you on an investment you know little or nothing about. How do you decide whether this investment is for you? Of course, knowing the source of the recommendation is important. Certainly you will not want to take the advice of someone whose reputation is unfamiliar or suspect. But, given a reputable source, how does one decide if this is the right investment for right now?

The problem with most individual investment suggestions is just that—they are individual, alone, unrelated to any overall plan or strategy. With stocks, for example, most recommendations are based on the merits of the particular company. Does the company seem to have favorable prospects? Are its earnings likely to increase in the future? Does the stock price seem low relative to the company's outlook? The two key elements we have stressed are often overlooked. First, does the risk entailed in this investment fit with the risk level most appropriate for you? Does it balance the risk of your portfolio in a manner you desire? Is it too risky, or not risky enough? This question can only be answered by you or someone very close to your financial situation. It is totally beyond the scope of a securities salesman who speaks to you on the phone once a year.

Second, the market outlook question must be answered. The stock recommendation is probably of interest only if the market outlook is favorable. While a handful of stocks may turn in acceptable performance in a declining market, the chances of being in the right stocks are slim. The problem is that the stock recommendation is probably being made by someone who specializes in a handful of stocks, not someone with a perspective on the overall market. The market outlook, the risk of the investment and how it relates to the risk of your portfolio must be answered before the merits of the stock can be considered.

While risk evaluation and forecasting the market outlook are crucial, most investment professionals have made and lost their reputations on their ability to pick stocks. Investment analysts who develop a track record for finding and recommending stocks that advance in price command high salaries. Their opinions are sought by investors everywhere. Everybody wants a big winner or two. Unfortunately, devoting all one's efforts to that end has led to many, many investment disasters. Eventually, hot analysts run into a slump, a couple of their recommendations flounder, and their reputations suddenly deteriorate. They are fighting the random walk in stock prices, the competition that comes from so much effort and attention devoted to finding attractive stocks, making it very difficult to succeed consistently.

Consequently, risk evaluation and determining the market outlook should take precedence. The main strategical objective should be to balance the portfolio at a risk level consistent with your personal preferences, your long-term financial requirements, and your market outlook. Then, invest in stocks with the goal of fully participating in the rising stock market that you expect. Stock selection should be the third step in the program. Not the primary question, but one of three.

Being the third step does not imply stock selection is unimportant. Far from it. The warning relates only to emphasis, since stock selection has been so seductive. Too many investors have had disastrous results by concentrating on stock selection to the detriment of risk evaluation and market timing. After the risk and outlook question are answered—and they need to be continually reappraised and reanswered—attention turns to stock selection.

THREE METHODS

There are as many approaches to stock selection as there are investors. No single approach is best for reasons already discussed, namely, the random walk argument. If there were a best method, everyone would use it. The method would defeat itself. Rather, investors need to be familiar with the basic techniques, then apply them with diligence and judgment.

Most techniques for picking stocks are variations of one of three methods—value, growth, and hot stocks. Value stocks are stocks that are selling at a low price compared to their true or intrinsic value. Essentially, they are bargains, marked down for quick sale. If a stock looks as though it's worth $50 per share but is currently trading at $25, it probably qualifies as undervalued. The danger here is that the stock may only appear to be worth $50. Just because you or I think it's worth $50 does not mean it has to sell at $50 in the immediate future. The stock may remain undervalued for a long time. Worse, the low price may be indicative of a deteriorating company that eventually is not worth even the $25.

Growth stocks are another approach. Basically, a growth stock is a stock that increases its earnings *per share* year after year at an above-average rate. Suppose over many years, the average company's earnings grow at, say, 6 percent per year. Companies that grow at 10 or 15 percent or more will likely be considered growth stocks. As we will show, companies that do grow at above-average rates over several years are indeed likely to prove to be good investments. However, picking growth stocks is much harder than it appears because some companies with apparently excellent prospects just do not grow.

The third method of stock selection is hot stocks that are currently favored by investors for one reason or another. Stock market interest tends to shift from one group of stocks to another for a variety of reasons. Investors who can guess the next shift in emphasis can profit greatly from the new trend. Those who stick with the old trend for too long can suffer painful losses. Staying in tune with the market can be a profitable technique for selecting stocks. It can also be dangerous.

Most stock selection techniques are variations of these three basic approaches. Technical analysts tend to fall in the hot stock camp, looking for stocks that are moving or about to move. Graham and Dodd epitomize the value approach, seeking sound companies at bargain basement prices. They have found that a diversified portfolio of cheap stocks usually holds a few that are eventually recognized by the stock market. This recognition provides enough performance to pull the overall portfolio into favorable territory. Growth-stock investing was, until 1974, considered the outstanding long-term approach to investment success. A number of growth stock-oriented investment firms had built up giant reputations through the 1960s and early 1970s. While selecting stocks that will grow, as opposed to those that have grown, is a difficult task, the more serious error of many growth-stock investors has been ignoring market timing.

One would suppose that the ideal stock is a low-priced growth stock in an area currently favored by the stock market. Obviously, such an outstanding combination of attractive characteristics is very difficult to find. Even if you find one, there is no guarantee of success, because many things can still go wrong. The market's attention may turn to another area, the growth may not prove as rosy as the prospects appear, and so forth. Nevertheless, a combination of value, growth potential, and market favor is a worthy goal.

Since the combination of all three is rare, investors usually have to settle for one of the three or perhaps a combination of two. This has led to complex ideologies regarding which characteristics and which combinations are more attractive. Are growth stocks better than value stocks? Are stocks in tune with the market better than either? Should one purchase a cheap growth stock, undervalued by the stock market, or a high-flying growth stock, overvalued but steadily moving to new highs? There is no answer. Some combinations work better at some times, others at other times. A portfolio will probably want to hold a diversity of the available combinations so as not to miss full participation in the overall market advance. Each approach has its season. Each must be understood by investors.

DETERMINING VALUE

The question "What is value?" has been debated by philosophers since the days of barter. Answers range from the academic view that current price is value to the more subtle answer that says value, like beauty, is in the eye of the beholder. It was not until the twentieth century that the philosophical subject of value could be reduced to formulas, or perhaps we should say, until men attempted to reduce value to formulas. As mentioned earlier, the colossal 778-page *Security Analysis* by Graham and Dodd is unquestionably the definitive work on the value of stocks.

Today, most value-oriented investors use methods outlined by Graham and Dodd. While the methods may not be perfect, the fact that so many use them provides credibility. If Technique 15b says that IBM is overvalued and millions of investors believe in Technique 15b, then IBM will probably act as though it is overvalued. The point being, it does not so much matter what Technique 15b is as it matters that so many use it.

One popular technique for determining value is based on a company's book value. This is simply the accounting value of the assets of the firm, less the accounting value of the firm's liabilities. True, Graham and Dodd would suggest a careful review of the accounting procedures used by the firm, for some accounting procedures are more liberal than others. Accounting, as you know, is not an exact science, but is subject to considerable interpretation. However, proper accounting should result in a proper book value, which in turn may have some relationship to the company's stock price. "Some relationship" is the correct term, because stocks seldom sell precisely at book value. Rather, the more consistent relationship is that some stocks usually sell well below their book value and others well above their book value.

The purist approach to selecting undervalued stocks is to find solid, financially sound companies with no accounting gimmicks selling at substantial discounts to book. XYZ Industries has a lot of cash, no debts, acres of timberland in Maine, a few buildings, a book value of $35 per share, and pays a good dividend. The stock is currently selling at $10. The stock is undervalued by almost any technique. An investor who buys shares will reap a large profit if the price ever approaches book value.

This value method is based on the ratio of price to book value. If the ratio is small, below 1.0, the stock is considered undervalued. A more popular approach is to use the stock's price to earnings ratio (P/E). Called the capitalization rate, P/E is important because it is related to yield. Actually, P/E is nothing more than earnings yield on an inverted scale. A P/E of 20 is an earnings yield (E/P) of 0.05, or 5 percent.

Over a period of years, many companies have tended to pay a reasonably steady proportion of their earnings out to shareholders in dividends. Since earnings are closely tied to dividends, earnings yield is closely related to dividend yield. P/E, being a form of earnings yield, is also closely tied to dividend yield. A high dividend yield (low P/E) is often a sign of an undervalued stock. If two stocks were identical in all respects except their stock price, the one with the lower price would have the superior dividend yield. Obviously, this stock is the undervalued of the two.

Of course, no two stocks are exactly alike, so determining undervaluation is more difficult. Two approaches are popular. The first compares a stock's current P/E with the same stock's P/E range over the past few years. Suppose a $25 stock has earnings per share of $2.50. The P/E is 10. Now take the high and low price for the stock for each of the last few years and relate each year's prices to earnings in that year. Is the stock's current P/E of 10 near or below the low P/Es of the last few years? If so, the stock may be undervalued.

P/E AND GROWTH

The second way to use P/E to determine value is to relate P/E to the stock's rate of growth of earnings per share. We are speaking here of future growth, not the historical record. We will deal with a method of forecasting growth in the next chapter. For the moment, our concern is valuation. The record clearly shows that stocks of companies that increase their earnings and dividends are worth more than stocks that do not. Growth adds to value, and rapid growth adds very substantially to value. This statement can be validated empirically and theoretically.

Historical results from the stock market show that at any point in time growth stocks command significantly higher prices than other stocks. Exhibit 6-1 shows groups of growth and nongrowth stocks as they appeared at the end of 1962. All the data have been adjusted for stock splits and stock dividends in the interim. On such relative value measures as yield and price/earnings ratio, the growth stocks were considerably more expensive in 1962 than the nongrowth stocks. In fact, some of the growth stocks were three to five times as expensive, because their P/Es were three to five times those of the nongrowth stocks.

Exhibit 6-2 shows that at the end of December 1972, 10 years later, growth stocks continued to appear more expensive in terms of lower dividend yield and higher price/earnings ratio.

Exhibit 6-3 relates the 1962 stock prices of these same growth stocks to 1972 dividends and earnings. On this basis, the comparison with nongrowth stocks is more favorable. The dividend yield on 1972 dividends compared to 1962 prices is 6.5 percent, far above the yield on nongrowth stocks. Similarly, the ratio of 1962 prices to 1972 earnings shows the growth stocks to have been outstanding values compared to the nongrowth stocks.

Apparently, 1962 purchasers of growth stocks were willing to pay a premium in yield and price/earnings ratio because they *foresaw* that earnings and dividends would grow to make future valuation comparisons more favorable. In fact, it took only a few years of growth before the dividends and earnings of the growth stocks appeared very inexpensive relative to the nongrowers.

The premium values of growth stocks rely on a prominent component of financial theory known as the "magic of compounding." Earnings that grow at an annual rate of, say, 15 percent, double every five years. Ten years from now they will be four times today's level; twenty years from now, sixteen times, and so forth. A small company, such as IBM was in the 1930s, can grow at a modest but steady rate for years and become one of the giants of industry and commerce. This growth justifies a high value even while the company is still small.

Certain factors, however, work against growth stock values. The growth stock investor must contend with the time value of money, which involves interest rates, and the fact that alternatives are available for employing his funds. He can, for example, put his money in a savings account and draw steady, assured interest. If the savings bank interest rate is 5 percent, one year from now he will have 1.05 times as much money as he has today. Two years from now he will have 1.05×1.05 or 1.1025 times as much as today, and so forth. In general, if the interest rate is r, after n years he will have $(1 + r)^n$ times as much as he does now. In other words, a dollar today can be converted into $1 + r$ dollars a year from now and $(1 + r)^n$ dollars n years from now.

Money has a time value, so that money received in the future is worth something less than money received now. If money received today can be multiplied by an interest rate factor to project it into the future, the lesser value of funds in the future can be evaluated in a similar manner.

EXHIBIT 6-1

20 Successful Growth Stocks as They Appeared in 1962

	1962 Price	1962 EPS	1962 P/E	1962 DPS	1962 Yield
Baxter Labs	$ 3	$ .13	24.0	$.03	1.2%
Marriott Corporation	2	.10	19.1	.00	0.0
Burroughs Corporation	14	.71	19.8	.50	3.6
Johnson & Johnson	8	.33	24.3	.11	1.4
Schering-Plough Corp.	5	.31	16.1	.19	3.8
Xerox Corporation	11	.24	44.0	.05	.4
Delta Air Lines	5	.37	14.6	.09	1.6
Evans Products Company	2	.04	50.0	.00	0.0
AMP	4	.20	20.9	.06	1.4
Avon Products	15	.44	33.1	.23	1.6
Schlumberger Limited	10	.62	15.7	.09	.9
Royal Crown Cola Company	6	.32	18.9	.18	3.0
Eli Lilly & Company	10	.40	24.9	.31	3.1
Merck & Company	13	.45	28.8	.30	2.3
Coca-Cola Company	21	.84	25.2	.60	2.8
Polaroid Corporation	18	.31	56.9	.02	.1
Eastman Kodak Company	26	.87	29.9	.55	2.1
American Home Products	9	.38	22.9	.26	2.9
IBM	81	2.28	35.6	.62	.8
Minnesota Mining & Mfg.	27	.80	32.9	.40	1.5
AVERAGE			27.9		1.7%

That is, saying that one dollar today is worth 1.05 dollars a year from now is the same as saying that $1.05 a year from now is worth $1 today. One multiplies by the interest rate factor $(1 + r)$ to project money into the future and divides by the interest rate factor $1/(1 + r)$ to discount future money back to today.

This is an important consideration for evaluating growth stocks because their highest earnings and dividends come in the distant

20 Nongrowth Stocks as They Appeared in 1962

	1962 Price	1962 EPS	1962 P/E	1962 DPS	1962 Yield
Ingersoll-Rand Company	$33	$2.05	16.2	$2.00	2.4%
Ford Motor Company	45	4.36	10.4	1.80	4.0
General Motors Corporation	58	5.10	11.4	3.00	5.2
International Harvester	25	1.93	12.9	1.20	4.8
Bethlehem Steel Corp.	29	1.80	15.9	2.18	7.6
B. F. Goodrich Company	29	1.91	14.9	1.47	5.1
Republic Steel Corp.	35	2.54	13.6	2.50	7.2
Reynolds Metals Company	24	1.35	17.6	0.50	2.1
CPC International	51	2.08	24.5	1.30	2.6
Penn-Dixie Industries	15	1.46	9.9	1.20	8.2
NL Industries	34	2.00	17.0	1.63	4.8
Wheeling Pittsburgh	27	2.54	10.5	1.50	5.6
Food Fair Stores	21	1.40	14.6	0.87	4.2
American Stores Company	51	3.77	13.6	1.35	2.6
Kaiser Aluminum & Chemical	35	1.74	20.3	0.90	2.5
Great Atlantic & Pacific	38	2.44	15.7	1.62	4.2
Scott Paper Company	33	1.23	26.5	0.80	2.5
American Motors Corp.	16	1.85	3.8	0.80	4.9
Falstaff Brewing Company	15	1.36	11.1	0.65	4.3
Marquette Cement Mfg.	37	3.11	11.8	1.80	4.9
		AVERAGE	14.9		4.71%

future. And the distant future is discounted considerably before it receives a value today. In the 1962 growth stock example, stock prices were relatively high compared to 1962 stock dividends. Eventually those dividends grew, so that by 1972 dividends and earnings were substantial, relative to 1962. To a 1962 investor, however, 1972 dividends were far in the future and were heavily discounted.

Based on these concepts, a simple formula for determining the value

EXHIBIT 6-2

20 Successful Growth Stocks as They Appeared in 1972

	1972 Price	1972 EPS	1972 P/E	1972 DPS	1972 Yield
Baxter Labs	$ 56	$0.77	72.4	$0.13	0.2%
Marriott Corporation	35	0.59	58.9	0.00	0.0
Burroughs Corporation	217	4.71	46.1	0.63	0.3
Johnson & Johnson	131	2.15	60.7	0.45	0.3
Schering-Plough Corp.	137	2.16	63.3	1.35	1.0
Xerox Corporation	149	3.16	47.2	0.84	0.6
Delta Air Lines	65	2.20	29.6	0.50	0.8
Evans Products Company	23	1.64	14.0	0.29	1.3
AMP	43	0.90	47.4	0.22	0.5
Avon Products	137	2.16	63.3	1.35	1.0
Schlumberger Limited	91	1.94	46.7	0.49	0.5
Royal Crown Cola Company	45	1.48	30.4	0.56	1.3
Eli Lilly & Company	80	1.85	43.0	0.73	0.9
Merck & Company	89	1.99	44.8	1.12	1.3
Coca-Cola Company	149	3.19	46.6	1.64	1.1
Polaroid Corporation	126	1.30	97.0	0.32	0.3
Eastman Kodak Company	148	3.39	43.8	1.39	0.9
American Home Products	41	1.08	37.7	0.59	1.5
IBM	322	8.82	36.5	4.32	1.3
Minnesota Mining & Mfg.	86	2.17	39.5	0.96	1.1
AVERAGE			47.6		.8%

of a stock can be derived. This derivation is contained in the Technical Appendix at the end of this chapter. Interested readers will find that only a knowledge of high school algebra is required.

Based on a formula derived in the appendix, Exhibit 6-4 charts value in relation to a stock's anticipated growth rate. (Value is shown as Price/Dividend, or P/D, rather than P/E, but the concepts are similar, as

20 Nongrowth Stocks as They Appeared in 1972

	1972 Price	1972 EPS	1972 P/E	1972 DPS	1972 Yield
Ingersoll-Rand Company	$66	$4.16	15.8	$2.08	3.2%
Ford Motor Company	80	8.52	9.4	2.67	3.4
General Motors Corporation	81	7.51	10.8	4.45	5.5
International Harvester	38	3.17	12.1	1.40	3.7
Bethlehem Steel Corp.	29	3.02	9.7	1.20	4.1
B. F. Goodrich Company	28	3.33	8.5	1.00	3.5
Republic Steel Corp.	26	2.66	9.7	1.25	4.8
Reynolds Metals Company	16	− .19	NA	0.45	2.8
CPC International	33	2.71	12.0	1.72	5.3
Penn-Dixie Industries	9	0.83	10.8	0.13	1.5
NL Industries	17	1.53	11.0	1.00	5.9
Wheeling Pittsburgh	20	2.78	7.3	0.00	0.0
Food Fair Stores	9	0.91	9.8	0.54	6.0
American Stores Company	24	1.03	23.2	1.50	6.3
Kaiser Aluminum & Chemical	18	0.62	28.6	0.50	2.8
Great Atlantic & Pacific	16	− 2.06	NA	0.60	3.7
Scott Paper Company	15	1.11	13.9	0.90	3.3
American Motors Corp.	8	0.64	12.9	0.00	0.0
Falstaff Brewing Company	5	− 1.35	NA	0.10	2.0
Marquette Cement Mfg.	11	0.32	33.6	0.00	0.0
	AVERAGE		14.1		3.4%

already noted.) Value increases very rapidly with higher projected earnings growth. Indeed, a high growth rate justifies a high valuation on a stock even if an investor requires a high rate of return on investment, called the discount rate here. This is theoretical confirmation of our earlier empirical result that high growth commands a high valuation.

EXHIBIT 6-3

20 Successful Growth Stocks
(1962 price compared with 1972 earnings and dividends)

	1962 Price	1972 EPS	P/E	1972 DPS	Yield
Baxter Labs	$ 3	$0.77	3.9	$0.13	4.5%
Marriott Corporation	2	0.59	3.4	0.00	0.0
Burroughs Corporation	14	4.71	3.0	0.63	4.5
Johnson & Johnson	8	2.15	3.7	0.45	5.5
Schering-Plough Corp.	5	2.16	2.3	1.35	9.4
Xerox Corporation	11	3.16	3.5	0.84	8.0
Delta Air Lines	5	2.20	2.3	0.50	9.4
Evans Products Company	2	1.64	1.2	0.29	13.5
AMP	4	0.90	4.4	0.22	5.2
Avon Products	15	2.16	6.9	1.35	9.3
Schlumberger Limited	10	1.94	5.2	0.49	5.1
Royal Crown Cola Company	6	1.48	4.1	0.56	9.4
Eli Lilly & Company	10	1.85	5.4	0.73	7.3
Merck & Company	13	1.99	6.5	1.12	8.7
Coca-Cola Company	21	3.19	6.6	1.64	7.7
Polaroid Corporation	18	1.30	13.8	0.32	1.8
Eastman Kodak Company	26	3.39	7.7	1.39	5.4
American Home Products	9	1.08	8.3	0.59	6.7
IBM	81	8.82	9.2	4.32	5.3
Minnesota Mining & Mfg.	27	2.17	12.4	0.96	3.6
		AVERAGE	5.7		6.5%

COMPARING STOCKS

Exhibit 6-4 showing value and growth, along with the mathematical formulas in the Technical Appendix, is a valid method of determining fair value only under certain very restrictive assumptions. The most important is that the projected growth rate will continue without interruption forever. While this assumption is altered later in the

20 Nongrowth Stocks

(1962 price compared with 1972 earnings and dividends)

	1962 Price	1972 EPS	P/E	1972 DPS	Yield
Ingersoll-Rand Company	$33	$4.16	7.9	$2.08	6.3%
Ford Motor Company	45	8.52	5.3	2.67	5.9
General Motors Corporation	58	7.51	7.7	4.45	7.7
International Harvester	25	3.17	7.9	1.40	5.6
Bethlehem Steel Corp.	29	3.02	9.6	1.20	4.2
B. F. Goodrich Company	29	3.33	8.7	1.00	3.5
Republic Steel Corp.	35	2.66	13.2	1.25	3.6
Reynolds Metals Company	24	−.19	NA	1.45	1.9
CPC International	51	2.71	18.8	1.72	3.4
Penn-Dixie Industries	15	0.83	18.1	0.13	0.9
NL Industries	34	1.53	22.2	1.00	2.9
Wheeling Pittsburgh	27	2.78	9.7	0.00	0.0
Food Fair Stores	21	0.91	23.1	0.54	2.6
American Stores Company	51	1.03	49.5	1.50	2.9
Kaiser Aluminum & Chemical	35	0.62	56.5	0.50	1.4
Great Atlantic & Pacific	38	−2.06	NA	0.60	1.6
Scott Paper Company	33	1.11	29.7	0.50	1.5
American Motors Corp.	16	0.64	25.0	0.00	0.0
Falstaff Brewing Company	15	−1.35	NA	0.10	0.7
Marquette Cement Mfg.	37	0.32	115.6	0.00	0.0
	AVERAGE		25.2		2.8%

appendix, it remains a difficult task for most investors to predict both the rate and pattern of future growth with sufficient accuracy to justify applying the mathematics. In some cases, the assumptions will be valid, and investors will have the computational power to do the arithmetic. Most, however, will find this an onerous task.

Consequently, a shorthand approach is suggested, which facilitates comparisons among stocks. Suppose an investor is interested in a

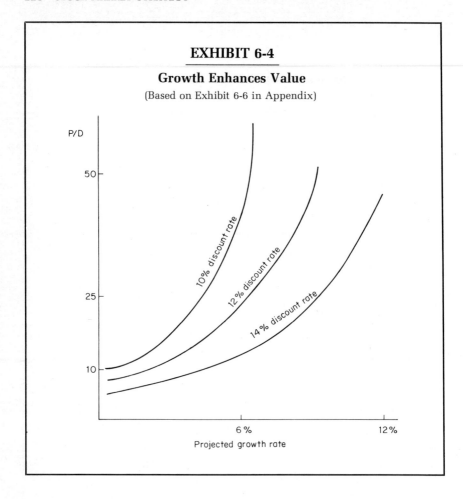

EXHIBIT 6-4

Growth Enhances Value

(Based on Exhibit 6-6 in Appendix)

group of stocks of varying P/Es and growth rates. Which of these stocks are likely to be the most undervalued? One approach is to chart the stocks as shown in Exhibit 6-5. Here each stock's ticker symbol is used to locate the stock on the chart. The vertical axis is P/E and the horizontal axis is your forecast of future growth rate. (A method of making growth forecasts will be outlined in the next chapter.)

Note that lower-growth stocks like T and GM tend to fall in the lower left corner as low growth usually means low P/E. On the other hand, stocks like DEC and MCD are in the upper right corner since anticipated high growth warrants a high P/E.

One way to determine which stocks are more undervalued is to draw

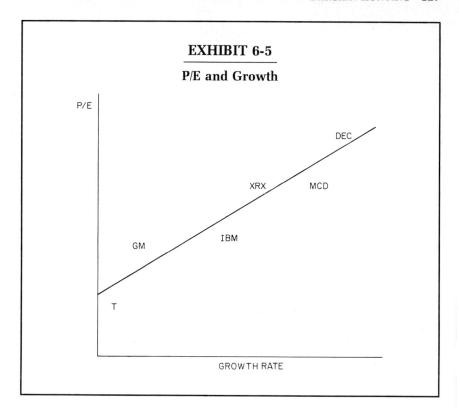

EXHIBIT 6-5

P/E and Growth

a line through the cluster of ticker symbols. The line should be sloping upward to the right (southwest to northeast) reflecting the positive relationship between P/E and growth. The exact placement and slope of the line is open to debate. Experience indicates that the best-fitting line tends to float between slopes of 1.0 and 2.0, depending on the stock market's current enthusiasm for growth.

Whichever line is chosen, the more undervalued securities lie below and to the right of the fair valuation line (southeast of the line). With these companies, one is paying a lower price (lower P/E) for a given level of projected growth.

Care must be exercised in applying this charting technique because it, too, incorporates some heroic assumptions. First, you must have some confidence in the earnings and growth forecasts used. Actually, you should have equal confidence in each forecast—lower degrees of confidence imply lower P/Es. Then, you must select the proper fair valuation line. Note that for simplicity we used a straight line in

Exhibit 6-5, while Exhibit 6-4 suggests a curve as more theoretically sound. Finally, growth is not the only factor to account for differences in P/E. Risk, capitalization, and other factors must be considered. Despite these handicaps, the charting technique often provides helpful insights into valuation.

CONCLUSION

Three basic methods of selecting stocks—value, growth, and hot stocks—were mentioned and value was reviewed in some detail. Growth stocks and hot stocks will be reviewed in the next two chapters. No single method is best, and few stocks are outstanding on all three characteristics. Judgment must be used in applying these techniques to stock selection. Most portfolios will want to hold stocks that are attractive on a diversity of characteristics in order to participate fully in the stock market's overall advance.

A checklist for determining whether a stock is undervalued would go something like this:

1. Obtain the stock's price, estimated earnings per share, dividends per share, book value per share, and estimated future growth rate.

2. Is price below book value? How does the current price to book value ratio (P/B) compare to this same ratio in prior years? (Some stocks tend to trade in a given P/B range, 0.75 to 1.50, for example.)

3. Compute the stock's high and low P/E in each of the last five years using the high price, low price, and earnings per share for each year. Is the current P/E high or low based on this record?

4. Make a P/E versus Growth Rate chart (Exhibit 6-5) including several stocks at various levels of growth potential. Draw in a fair value line sloping upward to the right. Does the stock's P/E appear low compared to this line?

A stock that passes all or most of these criteria is a bargain stock. This does not guarantee it will appreciate in price. There is no guarantee that an undervalued stock will be recognized by other investors. They may find its low price appropriate and leave you to languish with your dull stock. Similarly, there is no reason why an apparently overvalued stock must decline in price. It can remain overvalued for years simply because others do not agree that it is overvalued. Nevertheless, value is an important stock selection concept and should be applied as such.

TECHNICAL APPENDIX TO CHAPTER SIX
Valuation Formulas

Suppose a stock pays an annual dividend in the amount D_0 and this dividend is expected to remain fixed forever—no growth and no decline. The value of this stock can be determined by discounting each and every future dividend payment back to the present at the appropriate discount rate r.

Value = first year's dividend discounted at $1 + r$ plus second year's dividend discounted at $(1 + r)^2$ plus third dividend at $(1 + r)^3$, etc.

$$\text{Value} = \frac{D_0}{1 + r} + \frac{D_0}{(1 + r)^2} + \frac{D_0}{(1 + r)^3} + \frac{D_0}{(1 + r)^4} \cdots$$

This may appear complicated at first, but it turns out that the sum of $1/(1 + r)$, $1/(1 + r)^2$, and so on is simply $1/r$. So

$$\text{Value} = \frac{D_0}{r}$$

is the value of a stock paying a dividend of D_0 each year, forever.

The value of a growth stock can be calculated in an equally simple way. If a company's earnings and dividends are expected to grow forever at g percent per annum, the company's dividends in the future will be $D_0(1 + g)$, $D_0(1 + g)^2$, and so on. Thus, the value equation becomes:

$$\text{Value} = \frac{D_0(1 + g)}{1 + r} + \frac{D_0(1 + g)^2}{(1 + r)^2} + \frac{D_0(1 + g)^3}{(1 + r)^3} + \cdots$$

Again, mathematics comes to our aid as the equation reduces to:

$$\text{Value} = \frac{D_0}{r - g} \qquad \text{for } r > g$$

(This assumes that the growth rate which lasts forever is less than the discount rate r. Otherwise the value of the stock would be infinite.)

Exhibit 6-6 shows the effect of alternative discount rates r, and alternative perpetual growth rates g, on the value, or price, of a stock

EXHIBIT 6-6

Stock Prices with Various Growth Rates

D_0 = initial dividend = $1 per share

Growth Rate, %	Discount Rate		
	10%	12%	14%
0	$ 10.00	$ 8.33	$ 7.14
1	11.11	9.09	7.69
2	12.50	10.00	8.33
3	14.29	11.11	9.09
4	16.67	12.50	10.00
5	20.00	14.29	11.11
6	25.00	16.67	12.50
7	33.33	20.00	14.29
8	50.00	25.00	16.67
9	100.00	33.33	20.00
10	∞	50.00	25.00
11	∞	100.00	33.33
12	∞	∞	50.00

$$\text{Price} = \frac{D_0}{r - g} \qquad \text{for } r > g$$

whose current dividend is $1 per share. Moving down the columns vertically, note that a small increase in the growth rate implies a large increase in the value of the stock. One should be willing to pay a much higher price for a growth stock than for a nongrowth stock.[1]

The formula gets into difficulty as the growth rate approaches the discount rate. The assumption up to now has been perpetual growth at a certain rate, a vast simplification because no one expects any company, even IBM, to continue growing forever. Investment analysts frequently illustrate this point by noting that if IBM continued to grow

[1]For this exercise, we ignore the problem of selecting an appropriate discount rate. As we have seen, this rate should be consistent with the risk of the stock, greater risk requiring a higher rate of return (discount rate).

at a high rate, say, 10 to 15 percent per annum, it would not be very many years before the company was larger than the entire national economy.

The reasons for expecting any growth rate to slow are more human, and less theoretical, than this. The public eventually loses interest in any product, competition increases, managements become older and more cautious, big companies lose their dynamism, and government slows down monopolistic enterprises. Whatever the reasons, growth eventually slows to below the discount rate and all stocks have a finite value. Or, looked at another way, the stock market refuses to believe that any stock will grow forever, and so puts a finite value on all stocks. Consequently, one can think of stocks currently growing at a rate higher than the discount rate as having a period of supergrowth. This will eventually taper off to a more normal long-term rate, such as the rate of growth of the economy as a whole of, say, 6 percent or so.

The growth stock valuation equation can be rewritten to represent a period of supergrowth followed by perpetual growth at a slower rate. For example, given a discount rate of 12 percent, one might estimate

EXHIBIT 6-7a

Value of a Stock Paying $1 in Dividends for Various Rates and Durations of Supergrowth

(Discount rate = 10 percent)

Super-growth Rate, %	Years of Supergrowth			
	1	2	4	6
12	$26.47	$27.97	$31.05	$34.25
14	26.95	28.96	33.22	37.79
16	27.42	29.97	35.49	41.64
18	27.89	30.99	37.89	45.82
20	28.36	32.03	40.40	50.36
25	29.55	34.71	47.25	63.44
30	30.73	37.50	54.95	79.33

that a particular growth company will have a supergrowth rate of 15 percent for 10 years and a 6 percent growth rate thereafter.

We have already seen that the formula for the value of a constant growth rate in perpetuity is simply $D/(r - g)$. In this case, the perpetual growth value is out 10 years, so it's discounted by $1/(1 + r)^{10}$. We then have to calculate the present value of the dividends received during the 10 years of supergrowth. If the supergrowth rate is called s,

$$\text{Value} = \frac{D_0(1 + s)}{(1 + r)} + \cdots + \frac{D_0(1 + s)^{10}}{(1 + r)^{10}} + \left[\frac{1}{(1 + r)^{10}} \times \frac{D_0(1 + s)^{10}}{(r - g)} \right]$$

where the first terms represent the 10 years of supergrowth and the last term represents the value of the subsequent normal growth.

Exhibit 6-7 (a, b, c) shows the value of supergrowth for various growth rates and periods of time. Note that under these assumptions, high levels of growth for long periods result in very high current prices. For example, using a discount rate of 10 percent, a stock that could be expected to grow at 14 percent for 20 years would be worth a

8	10	15	20
$37.56	$ 40.99	$ 50.14	$ 60.14
42.70	47.97	62.92	80.79
48.47	56.07	79.00	108.91
54.95	65.46	99.19	147.10
62.22	76.33	124.47	198.85
84.35	111.36	218.47	421.43
113.37	160.92	379.49	883.37

EXHIBIT 6-7b

Value of a Stock Paying $1 in Dividends for Various Rates and Durations of Supergrowth

(Discount rate = 12 percent)

Super-growth Rate, %	Years of Supergrowth			
	1	2	4	6
12	$17.67	$18.67	$20.67	$22.67
14	17.98	19.32	22.07	24.92
16	18.30	19.99	23.55	27.37
18	18.61	20.66	25.10	30.03
20	18.93	21.35	26.73	32.91
25	19.72	23.12	31.16	41.18
30	20.51	24.96	36.14	51.20

EXHIBIT 6-7c

Value of a Stock Paying $1 in Dividends for Various Rates and Durations of Supergrowth

(Discount rate = 15 percent)

Super-growth Rate, %	Years of Supergrowth			
	1	2	4	6
12	$11.80	$12.46	$13.74	$14.96
14	12.01	12.89	14.64	16.36
16	12.22	13.33	15.59	17.89
18	12.43	13.78	16.58	19.54
20	12.64	14.23	17.63	21.33
25	13.16	15.40	20.46	26.44
30	13.69	16.61	23.63	32.61

8	10	15	20
$24.67	$26.67	$ 31.67	$ 36.67
27.87	30.93	39.07	47.96
31.47	35.86	48.30	63.13
35.49	41.56	59.81	83.51
39.99	48.13	74.14	110.85
53.65	69.19	126.86	226.71
71.48	98.81	216.17	463.43

8	10	15	20
$16.11	$17.20	$ 19.69	$ 21.88
18.05	19.72	23.74	27.60
20.23	22.61	28.74	35.14
22.65	25.93	34.90	45.10
25.35	29.74	42.48	58.25
33.51	41.86	69.97	112.63
44.07	58.73	115.75	220.99

fantastic $80.79 per dollar of current dividends—but it would provide a current dividend yield of only 1.2 percent. Yet, under these assumptions, an investor could pay up to $80.79 per dollar of current dividends and receive a total return of 10 percent per annum by holding this stock forever.

SEVEN
Growth Stocks[1]

THE MYSTIQUE OF GROWTH STOCKS

Everyone is familiar with growth stocks. You buy them at a premium price, hold them for several years as earnings grow, in spite of recessions and the like, and make a phenomenal return on your investment. According to investment advisors who specialize in growth stocks, and there are many, the price of a growth stock always seems high. But don't worry. Buying it and putting it away assures an eventual profit as earnings growth devours whatever price premium you may have thought was present. The trick is to select good quality growth stocks and have patience. The uncertainties of the market, the economy, politics, and international developments may have a short-term impact on the price of your growth stock, but over the long run, earnings growth will pull you through.

IBM is the classic growth stock, the epitome of every quality that growth-stock lovers dream of. Exhibit 7-1 shows the earnings per share growth of IBM from 1954 to 1974. On a logarithmic scale, earnings per share are almost a straight line. IBM has been a real growth stock: consistent, predictable growth, decade after decade.

IBM is not the only growth stock, nor is it even the one that has done the best for its shareholders in the last decade. Names like American Home Products, Avon, Coca-Cola, Eastman Kodak, First National City

---

[1]An earlier version of this chapter was published in the Fall 1974 *Journal of Portfolio Management*, Peter Bernstein, Editor, under the title, "You Cannot Live with One Decision."

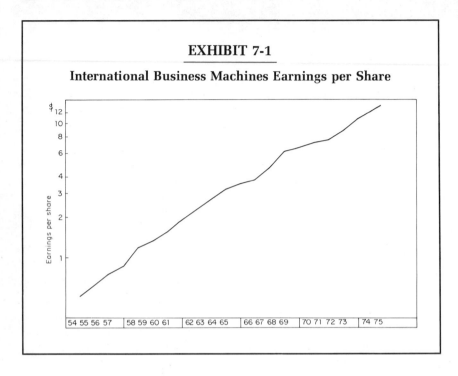

EXHIBIT 7-1

International Business Machines Earnings per Share

Bank, Kresge, Merck, MMM, Procter & Gamble, Sears, and Xerox have all been growth stocks in the IBM tradition.

What distinguishes this list of stocks has been their ability to increase earnings at a far more rapid rate than other companies. The continual compounding of earnings per share has pushed their stock prices far above levels of a decade ago, providing substantial returns to their shareholders, captivating the interest of the stock market, and making these stocks outstanding investments.

Exhibit 7-2 illustrates the relationship between earnings growth and stock price appreciation over a period of several years. Exhibit 7-2 shows the stock price appreciation of 20 stocks whose earnings have grown substantially from 1962 to 1972, and the same data for a group of 20 well-known stocks whose earnings growth has been substandard over the same period. The difference is striking. The growth stocks returned an average of 26.4 percent per year compared to 0.9 percent per year from the nongrowth stocks. During this same period, the Standard & Poor's 500 stock index had a total return (price appreciation plus dividends) of about 9.3 percent per year.

On the basis of these data, it appears that the stock market investment problem has been solved. All you do is find a few growth stocks, buy them, and forget them, because in the long run you are virtually guaranteed a comfortable rate of return on your investments. You have to make just one decision: Is this a growth stock or not? And with the assistance of today's high-powered security analysts and portfolio managers, that decision should not be difficult. Then you can rest securely on the conviction that long-term earnings growth will assure a nice rate of return. Just ignore short-term stock market fluctuations which have a minor effect on the value of your growth stock holdings. Make that one decision, make it correctly, and you are all set.

This may seem a vast oversimplification of a complex investment philosophy, but it is widely accepted in the investment community as truth. Just read the investment philosophy or investment strategy statements of some leading investment advisors and mutual fund management companies.

> Over the years we have found that a company which meets the various (growth stock) requirements will grow faster than the economy. Its common stock will fluctuate with the . . . general market. But its sales and earnings, and the market value of its shares can be expected to reach new high levels at the peak of each succeeding business cycle.

> . . . we don't know of a single investor who has been successful over the years because of his ability to forecast short-term developments. On the other hand, many individuals and institutions have achieved above average investment results by basing their policy on long-range (i.e., growth stock) trends.

> Our current investment policy is basically oriented towards quality-growth common stocks, consistent with our belief that this type of investment will produce superior results over the long-term. . . . We believe that preoccupation with the current market sentiments and attempts to exercise overly-precise price judgments are detrimental . . .

> At the heart of our philosophy is our belief that, in the long run, shares of companies with superior earnings growth . . . will eventually reflect this growth in superior market performance.

While the virtues of growth stocks are widely extolled in the investment community, the facts do not support the conclusions. Growth stocks are not what their proponents say they are. Simply put, growth

EXHIBIT 7-2

Performance of 20 Successful Growth Stocks, 1962–72

	1962 Price	1972 Price	EPS Growth	1962–72 Total Return
Baxter Labs	$ 3	$ 56	22.5%	34.7%
Marriott Corporation	2	35	19.5	33.5
Burroughs Corporation	14	217	25.0	32.9
Johnson & Johnson	8	131	20.7	32.8
Schering-Plough Corp.	5	69	16.7	32.0
Xerox Corporation	11	149	27.5	31.4
Delta Air Lines	5	65	16.0	30.5
Evans Products Company	2	23	21.9	29.7
AMP	4	43	15.3	26.9
Avon Products	15	137	17.1	26.9
Schlumberger Limited	10	91	12.6	26.2
Royal Crown Cola	6	45	11.4	25.4
Eli Lilly & Company	−10	80	17.2	25.0
Merck & Company	13	89	15.0	23.9
Coca-Cola Company	21	149	14.0	23.7
Polaroid Corporation	18	126	18.7	21.9
Eastman Kodak Company	26	148	14.1	20.9
American Home Products	9	41	11.1	18.9
IBM	81	322	14.6	16.2
Minnesota Mining & Mfg.	27	86	10.2	14.0
		AVERAGE	17.0%	26.4%
S&P 500				9.3%

stocks do not have the wonderful characteristics their supporters would have us believe. The whole growth-stock mystique is an over-simplified approach to investment that cannot and does not work. Worse, this philosophy leads to incorrect use of growth stocks in investment portfolios.

Growth-stock proponents are incorrect on several points. First,

Performance of 20 Nongrowth Stocks

	1962 Price	1972 Price	EPS Growth	1962–72 Total Return
ıgersoll-Rand Company	$33	$66	6.8%	11.7%
ord Motor Company	45	80	4.1	9.8
eneral Motors Corporation	58	81	−9.9	9.8
ıternational Harvester	25	38	−1.6	9.7
ethlehem Steel Corp.	29	29	2.8	5.6
. F. Goodrich Company	29	28	−0.1	5.0
epublic Steel Corp.	35	26	−14.2	3.9
eynolds Metals Company	24	16	−9.5	0.0
PC International	51	33	1.5	−0.5
enn-Dixie Industries	15	9	−8.9	−0.7
L Industries	34	17	−5.5	−0.9
Vheeling Pittsburgh	27	20	−5.3	−2.0
ood Fair Stores	21	9	−0.3	−2.2
merican Stores Company	51	24	−5.3	−2.7
aiser Aluminum & Chemical	35	18	−2.7	−3.2
reat Atlantic & Pacific	38	16	−7.9	−3.2
cott Paper Company	33	15	−2.5	−3.4
merican Motors Corp.	16	8	−16.3	−4.4
alstaff Brewing Corp.	15	5	−19.9	−5.8
1arquette Cement Mfg.	37	11	−23.5	−8.6
		AVERAGE	−5.5%	.9%
&P 500				9.3%

strictly speaking, all stocks are growth stocks—at least all stocks whose current dividend yield is less than the interest rate on long-term corporate bonds. Second, there is no evidence that anyone has consistently bought and held growth stocks for long periods and significantly beaten the popular stock market averages. Even the growth-stock mutual funds substantially alter their portfolios as their evaluation of the likelihood of continued growth in a particular company changes. Third, with growth stocks, as with other stocks, market timing is extremely important. Buying growth stocks without regard to the market outlook—a tactic recommended by many growth-stock advocates— is a strategy that takes unnecessary risks and is likely to result in disappointing investment returns.

However, when used properly in investment portfolios, growth stocks can be a powerful positive factor. Our objective is to determine the proper role for growth stocks, taking into account the important factors we have already mentioned. On the dimension of risk evaluation, many outstanding growth stocks have moderate risk levels, making them suitable for a wide spectrum of investors. From a market-timing perspective, growth stocks have a degree of consistency of behavior in regard to the overall market cycle that can be of some assistance in improving investment performance. Of course, from the viewpoint of stock selection, value and investor interest must be considered along with growth characteristics.

PICKING GROWTH STOCKS IS NOT EASY

One reason many investors are so fond of growth stocks is that high growers are defined by hindsight. We all know that IBM, Xerox, Kodak, and others are growth stocks because they *have been*. Their earnings have grown, their stock prices have appreciated, and they command high stock prices today because the market expects earnings to continue to grow in the future. When investors talk of growth stocks, they usually think only of past winners. No one remembers the failures that fell by the wayside.

We have demonstrated that stocks whose earnings and dividends do grow are worth more. Investors should be willing to pay higher prices and accept a lower current income. But what about those stocks investors thought would grow, paid a high price to acquire, and then saw falter as earnings slipped and stock prices fell precipitously?

In an attempt to evaluate what happens to the stocks investors consider to be growth stocks *when* they buy them—not later when their performance is known—the holdings of 10 leading mutual funds in 1962 were studied. The growth funds used in this study are listed in Exhibit 7-4. Since these mutual funds were well known in 1972, they must have been reasonably successful in their stock selections over the years, including 1962. The assumption is that stocks owned by several of these growth-oriented mutual funds must have been considered growth stocks by investors as a group at that time. The phrase "at that time" is particularly important, because today everyone *knows* that some of these stocks were not growth stocks. The issue is what investors considered growth in 1962, without the benefit of hindsight.

The 1962–72 test period is particularly favorable for the growth-stock case. Growth stocks were at a relatively low-priced level at the end of 1962, having taken a severe beating in the 1962 market decline. Growth stocks were receiving premium valuations at the end of 1972 for reasons that will be discussed later. In short, growth stocks were probably undervalued in 1962 and overvalued in 1972, which should bias our results *in favor* of growth stocks.

The criterion for identifying 1962 growth stocks was ownership by three or more of these 10 growth mutual funds. The assumption is that this breadth of ownership represented a 1962 consensus judgment by knowledgeable investment managers that these stocks were genuine growth stocks. Forty-six stocks met this criterion, and their total returns (price appreciation plus dividend income) from 1962 to 1972 are shown in Exhibit 7-3. The total return from the S&P 500 stock index is also shown. Note that the consensus growth stocks selected by the funds did beat the S&P 500 stock index. The growth stocks provided an average return of 10.7 percent per annum compared to 9.3 percent from the S&P 500 index. While this appears to substantiate the claim that growth stocks are superior investments, the margin of superiority is only 1.4 percentage points per annum—a very modest margin considering that these stocks were selected by funds that by hindsight were highly successful in the years after 1962.

From a statistical point of view, this 1.4 percent margin is small compared to the variability of returns within the growth-stock sample. The returns range from Xerox's 31.4 percent per year, 22.1 percentage points better than the S&P 500, to Lockheed's −8.2 percent, 17.5 percentage points worse than the S&P 500. The 1.4 percentage point growth-stock margin is minuscule in this context. If just one of the big winners among the 46 growth stocks had been a failure, the margin of superiority would have disappeared. Looking at the results another way, only 48 percent, or 22 of the 46 growth stocks, beat the S&P 500 in the next decade. This is not a very impressive performance for the consensus holdings of funds that later proved themselves successful.

One could argue that the sample of 1962 growth stocks is not representative, even though they were owned by some of the leading

EXHIBIT 7-3

Performance of 1962 Consensus Growth Stocks
(Ranked by total return)

	Price 1962	Price 1972	Total Return 1962–72
Xerox Corporation	$ 11	$149	31.4%
Avon Products	15	137	26.9
American Greetings	6	48	25.2
Northwest Airlines	5	36	25.1
Merck & Company	13	89	23.8
Coca-Cola	21	149	23.7
Whirlpool Corporation	6	36	23.5
Polaroid Corporation	18	126	21.9
Eastman Kodak Company	26	148	20.9
Burlington Industries	13	37	16.2
International Business Mach.	81	322	16.2
ACF Industries	19	48	16.2
Pepsico	24	87	16.1
First National Citicorp.	11	38	15.4
Bristol-Myers Company	22	69	14.4
Minnesota Mining & Mfg.	27	86	14.0
International Tel. & Tel.	21	60	13.4
Pfizer	16	43	12.6
Coastal States Gas Corp.	12	35	11.3
Sunbeam Corporation	17	34	10.2
Ford Motor Company	45	80	9.8
General Motors Corporation	58	81	9.8
Rohm & Haas Company	42	89	8.9
Southern Pacific Company	29	44	8.9
Exxon Corporation	60	88	8.8

	Price 1962	Price 1972	Total Return 1962–72
Royal Dutch Petroleum	$ 26	$ 40	8.8%
Gulf Oil Corporation	20	27	8.3
Hercules	21	36	7.7
Reynolds Industries	42	52	6.7
United Aircraft Corporation	35	45	6.7
International Nickel	25	32	6.6
Texaco	29	38	6.6
Donnelley & Sons	15	21	5.2
Arkansas Louisiana Gas	28	27	4.6
Florida Power & Light	34	39	3.9
Union Carbide Corporation	50	50	3.8
American Electric Power	34	30	3.3
American Tel. & Telegraph	58	53	3.1
Tampa Electric Company	21	21	3.0
Pitney-Bowes	20	19	2.4
Virginia Electric & Power	30	22	.8
W. R. Grace & Company	39	27	.2
du Pont	240	178	−.2
Addressograph-Multigraph	51	33	−1.4
Scott Paper Company	33	15	−3.4
Lockheed Aircraft Company	41	9	−8.2
		AVERAGE	10.7%
S&P 500 Index			9.3%

institutional investors; or, perhaps the performance of the overall list is held down by a few stocks that were not "quality growth" stocks. This case can be made for one or two stocks in our sample. Ford, for example, was probably held in order to provide dividend income and broad market representation, not because it was seen as another IBM. But Ford didn't do that poorly in terms of total return. Lockheed is another stock that might be disputed, and its performance was rather poor. But 1962 was the height of the space race and right in the middle of rapid growth in commercial airlines. Perhaps investors did consider Lockheed a growth stock and simply were wrong.

Exhibit 7-4 shows the performance of each of the 10 growth mutual funds whose holdings were considered in developing the sample as

EXHIBIT 7-4

Performance of Growth Mutual Funds
1962–72

	Total Return 1962–72
Chase Fund of Boston	12.7%
Chemical Fund	13.7
Colonial Growth Shares	10.5
Investment Company of America	12.4
Johnston Mutual Fund	14.0
Massachusetts Investors Growth Stock Fund	10.7
Oppenheimer Fund	14.4
Penn Square Mutual Fund	13.0
T. Rowe Price Growth Fund	12.7
Putnam Growth Fund	11.2
AVERAGE	12.5%
S&P 500 Index	9.3%
Average total return of 1962 consensus growth stocks	10.7%

well as the average performance of their growth-stock selections. Note that the funds outperformed the market—which is one of the reasons they were selected for the study.

Of more interest, however, is the fact that the mutual funds also outperformed their consensus 1962 growth-stock holdings. This could be caused by any of several factors. Perhaps their nonconsensus holdings did better than the consensus growth stocks; perhaps it is a matter of portfolio weighting; or, more likely, that the funds were successful in weeding out the nongrowth stocks from their portfolios and reinvesting in new growth-stock selections. This in itself is a blow to the buy-and-hold growth-stocks theory. Even growth stocks require two decisions—when to buy and when to sell.

HIGH P/E STOCKS

Another approach to selecting stocks that were considered growth issues at an earlier time is to look at the stocks that sold at the highest relative valuations. The stocks with the highest price/earnings ratios in 1962 probably received their high multiples because investors expected their earnings to grow rapidly in the future. High P/Es, of course, may result from other factors—unusually depressed earnings or an asset valuation on the stock, for example. But a review of the stocks selected on a P/E basis (Exhibits 7-6, 7-7, and 7-8) indicates that such factors were not significant in this study.

If growth stocks are superior investments and P/E ratio is a measure of investor expectations of future growth, the higher P/E stocks should turn in superior performance. Not in every case, of course, but on average, high P/E stocks should be high-growth stocks and, according to growth-stock advocates, high-growth stocks should, in the aggregate, be superior investments.

This hypothesis was evaluated by dividing the 500 stocks in the S&P 500 index into 10 groups on the basis of 1962 P/E ratios. For this exercise, we defined the 1962 P/E as 1962 closing price divided by 1962 earnings. (Actually, earnings for only three of the four calendar 1962 quarters would have been known by investors at year-end 1962, so we are assuming perfect forecasting ability for the fourth quarter.) The first group (first decile) contained one-tenth of the companies in the S&P 500 stock index, the tenth with the highest P/Es in 1962. The second

---

EXHIBIT 7-5

Earnings Growth and Rate of Return for 1962 P/E Deciles

	1962 P/E Decile	EPS Growth 1962–72	Rate of Return 1962–72	Rate of Return Rank
Highest P/Es	1	10.6%	12.3%	4
	2	5.8	9.8	9
	3	7.2	10.6	7
	4	6.3	10.2	8
	5	5.6	10.7	6
	6	4.9	9.7	10
	7	7.7	14.1	1
	8	5.4	12.6	3
Lowest P/Es	9	5.3	13.5	2
	10	0.3	11.0	5
	AVERAGE	5.9%	11.5%	

---

decile contained the second highest 1962 P/Es, and the tenth decile contained the stocks in the S&P 500 with the lowest 1962 P/Es. According to the hypothesis, the first decile with the highest P/E, highest expected growth stocks should outperform the second decile, and so forth, with the tenth decile, composed of the lowest P/E, lowest-growth stocks, turning in the poorest performance. One should not expect perfect rank ordering of subsequent performance. But, at least in the aggregate, the higher P/E deciles containing the alleged growth stocks should outperform the lower P/E deciles.

Exhibit 7-5 shows the results of this analysis, comparing the 1962–1972 investment returns (dividend income plus price appreciation) of each P/E decile. Note that the highest P/E decile, containing the stocks 1962 investors must have expected to show significant earnings growth, did provide excellent investment returns, 12.3 percent per annum, on average. This is slightly above the 11.5 percent per annum average of the 10 deciles, that is, the entire sample.[2] However, the highest P/E decile provided only the fourth largest overall investment return for the 1962–1972 period. The second decile was ninth, or next to last, in performance. Most surprising is the fact that the four lowest P/E deciles, the stocks that 1962 investors apparently felt had little prospect for earnings growth, were four of the five best-return deciles, with deciles 7, 8, and 9 actually outperforming the highest P/E deciles.

Exhibit 7-5 also suggests that, aside from the extreme deciles (one and ten), 1962 investors had little ability to discriminate between stocks whose earnings would grow, and those whose earnings would not grow. As expected, the highest P/E decile provided the best earnings growth over the 1962–1972 period (10.6 percent per annum) and the lowest P/E decile had the poorest earnings growth (0.3 percent per annum). But the intermediate groups (two through nine) showed no consistent pattern of subsequent earnings growth.

Exhibits 7-6, 7-7, and 7-8 show three deciles of particular interest. Exhibit 7-6 lists the highest P/E decile, which contains such successful growth stocks as IBM, Xerox, Avon, Merck, Texas Instruments, and Polaroid. But it also includes several stocks that failed to live up to investor expectations: Litton, Varian, National Cash Register, and Corning Glass, for example. This latter group illustrates the point that growth stocks are hard to pick. Many of the stocks that 1962 investors expected to grow rapidly, as evidenced by the P/E they were willing to pay, simply did not grow. Consequently, their returns were disappointing.

Exhibit 7-7 is a list of stocks in the P/E decile with the best 1962–1972 investment returns. Actually, this is the decile with the seventh highest P/E, and it contains many stocks that 1962 investors obviously never expected to be outstanding performers. Kresge, with the highest

[2]The reader will note a difference between the 1962–1972 returns from the S&P 500 stock index (9.3 percent per annum) and the average of the sample of S&P 500 stocks in Exhibit 7-5 (11.5 percent per annum). There are several factors which account for this difference. The S&P 500 index is value weighted; our sample gives equal weight to each stock. Standard & Poor's Corporation changes the composition of the S&P 500 index from time to time; our sample is taken from the S&P 500 as it was constituted in March 1974. Finally, our sample contains only those S&P 500 stocks for which price and dividend data from 1962 to 1972 are available on the Compustat data tapes, a total of about 400 stocks. The significance of these and other differences was not investigated. As a result, Exhibits 7-5 to 7-8 are dependent on a consistent sample. Comparisons within Exhibits 7-5, 7-6, 7-7, and 7-8 are relevant. Comparisons with other samples and with popular stock market indices should be made with caution.

EXHIBIT 7-6

First 1962 P/E Decile
(Highest P/Es)

	EPS Growth 1962–72	Total Return 1962–72
Xerox Corporation	27.5%	31.4%
Evans Products Company	21.9	29.7
Avon Products	17.1	26.9
Holiday Inns	29.7	26.3
Merck & Company	15.0	23.8
Texas Instruments	12.8	22.8
American Hospital Supply	16.2	21.9
Polaroid Corporation	18.7	21.9
St. Joe Minerals	16.6	21.1
Eastman Kodak Company	14.1	20.9
Joy Manufacturing Company	16.9	19.8
International Business Mach.	14.6	16.2
ARA Services	12.9	16.0
G. D. Searle & Company	8.6	14.9
Bristol-Myers Company	13.3	14.4
Sperry Rand Corporation	17.0	14.3
Minnesota Mining & Mfg.	10.2	14.0
Procter & Gamble Company	9.9	13.9
Campbell Red Lake Mining	5.1	12.9
Control Data Corporation	26.7	12.6

return, was a second-rate retailer in 1962. Its 1962 dividend yield was 7 percent—hardly a growth-stock candidate. Schlitz and Halliburton are two other surprises from 1962. Little noticed then, they are considered respectable growth stocks today.

Exhibit 7-8 contains the lowest P/E decile. It turned in the poorest earnings growth, but ranks fifth in investment performance and contains several stocks—unknown in 1962—that later earned the accolade

	EPS Growth 1962–72	Total Return 1962–72
McCrory Corporation	22.5%	11.7%
UAL	3.7	11.3
Potlatch Corporation	8.1	9.6
General Electric Company	5.7	9.1
Metro-Goldwyn-Mayer	7.5	8.5
Owens-Corning-Fiberglas	6.5	8.5
Alberto Culver Company	12.6	8.4
Questor Corporation	7.1	7.5
Leesona Corporation	9.2	7.0
Corning Glass Works	4.0	6.9
Brown Company	−5.8	4.4
Campbell Soup Company	4.3	3.3
Purex Corporation	5.6	2.3
Gamble Skogmo	6.9	1.3
National Cash Register	−14.6	−.3
Beckman Instruments	0.8	−0.6
Scott Paper Company	−2.5	−3.4
Varian Associates	−2.4	−5.8
Litton Industries	9.3	−6.3
AVERAGE	10.6%	12.3%

"growth stock." Kaufman & Broad is an example, although it has had difficulties subsequent to 1972. On the whole, this tenth decile constitutes what even today would be considered a very speculative list, a judgment that again emphasizes how much investors are affected by past rather than future earnings growth.

This analysis is not intended as a review of stock selection on the basis of P/E or value alone. Based on empirical results similar to our P/E

EXHIBIT 7-7

Seventh 1962 P/E Decile
(Highest returns, 1962–72)

	EPS Growth 1962–72	Total Return 1962–72
S. S. Kresge Company	27.2%	47.1%
Joseph Schlitz Brewing	14.7	32.3
Halliburton Company	13.0	29.5
Fedders Corporation	20.2	27.5
Jim Walter Corporation	16.9	25.4
Mercantile Stores	15.0	23.9
W. T. Grant Company	12.1	21.5
Coca-Cola Bottling	15.7	20.1
Gardner-Denver Company	10.1	18.2
Time, Inc.	3.1	16.9
ACF Industries	4.4	16.2
American Broadcasting	7.7	15.8
R. H. Macy & Company	10.2	15.8
North American Coal Corp.	5.1	15.5
Rexnord	5.9	15.3
Norton Simon	11.8	15.2
Champion Spark Plug	10.1	14.9
Columbia Broadcasting	4.2	14.6
Foster Wheeler Corporation	14.5	14.4
American Smelting & Refining	9.8	14.4

decile analysis, some investment analysts have recommended bargain hunting among low P/E stocks. A correct evaluation of that subject would require careful attention to factors such as dropouts from the sample. The purpose here is only to stress that picking growth stocks and holding them for long periods is a difficult and uncertain path to investment success.

Growth stocks as a group have not provided superior returns because

	EPS Growth 1962–72	Total Return 1962–72
Chicago Pneumatic Tool	3.0%	11.5%
Sunbeam Corporation	1.4	10.2
Bendix Corporation	3.5	9.9
International Harvester	−1.6	9.7
Phelps Dodge Corporation	8.2	9.6
Continental Can	7.7	9.4
Mattel	12.1	9.0
Southern Pacific Company	5.6	8.9
National Distillers	3.1	8.7
Standard Oil Company	5.0	7.6
Brunswick Corporation	21.8	7.5
Scott, Foresman & Company	4.1	7.2
Cluett, Peabody & Company	.8	7.2
Reynolds Industries	6.1	6.7
Celanese Corporation	.8	5.4
Inland Steel Company	−1.5	4.1
Republic Steel Corporation	−14.2	3.9
Revere Copper & Brass	−2.8	1.4
GAC Corporation	7.1	−3.1
AVERAGE	7.7%	14.1%

some growth stocks just do not grow. Investors have considerable difficulty separating stocks that will compound their sales and earnings at an above-average rate, from those that will falter. Take, for example, the growth stocks listed in Exhibit 7-3 that were selected by mutual funds in 1962. In the next 10 years, these stocks had an average annual growth rate in earnings per share of 6.6 percent, quite in line with the growth of the average stock in the S&P 500 index. In other

EXHIBIT 7-8

Tenth 1962 P/E Decile
(Lowest P/Es)

	EPS Growth 1962-72	Total Return 1962-72
Kaufman & Broad	28.1%	47.0%
Reading & Bates Offshore	4.1	23.1
J. Ray McDermott & Company	−.9	19.1
Getty Oil Company	8.2	18.9
Mohasco Industries	8.5	17.9
Akzona	6.2	17.9
Deere & Company	4.4	17.6
Trans World Airlines	−20.6	16.8
Reeves Brothers	13.5	16.7
National Can Corporation	14.9	16.5
Atlantic Richfield Company	5.5	16.3
Burlington Industries	1.8	16.2
Warner & Swasey Company	−5.2	16.1
Giddings & Lewis	15.9	15.1
Chrysler Corporation	−2.2	14.0
Koehring Company	−8.1	12.2
General Development Corp.	29.4	10.6
Monarch Machine Tool Company	−18.4	10.6
General Instrument Corp.	−.5	10.5
Eastern Air Lines	−22.2	10.0
Brown & Sharpe Manufacturing	−16.2	9.9

words, these alleged growth stocks had about the same growth rate as any random sample of stocks in 1962.

In short, predicting future earnings growth is extremely difficult. As a result, most lists of growth stocks contain many nongrowers as well. And that includes growth-stock lists prepared by the most knowledgeable professional investors.

	EPS Growth 1962–72	Total Return 1962–72
Massey Ferguson Limited	−5.6%	9.4%
Pan American World Airways	16.7	8.9
Interlake	1.7	8.6
J. P. Stevens & Company	−4.7	8.5
Flintkote Company	−.2	8.3
Anaconda Company	1.8	8.0
Budd Company	3.9	7.6
Sonesta International Hotels	4.3	7.0
Twentieth Century-Fox	−9.9	6.1
Holly Sugar Corporation	−7.6	5.9
SCM Corporation	2.7	5.8
Chris Craft Industries	6.1	5.6
Kayser-Roth Corporation	2.6	5.1
White-Motor Corporation	−15.1	4.3
Copper Range Company	14.2	3.4
Alpha Portland Industries	−6.4	2.7
General Dynamics Corporation	−13.8	.9
Penn-Dixie Industries	−8.9	−.7
Great Western United Corp.	0.0	−2.2
American Motors Corporation	−16.3	−4.4
AVERAGE	0.3%	11.0%

GROWTH STOCKS AND MARKET TIMING

The most erroneous tenet of the growth-stock investment philosophy, at least in its simplest form, says that market timing is not important. In this view, stock market fluctuations are an imponderable that cannot be predicted and, over the long term, can be ignored. One's favorite growth stocks can take a little beating in the market now and then. But over the long pull, they will surely come back, and we will be better off than other investors who tried to play every little swing in the market.

The trouble with this argument is that growth stocks do not always provide superior returns over the long term, as was shown in the previous section. In addition, short-term swings in growth stocks can be substantial, in a few weeks wiping out the accumulated gains of several years.

Exhibit 7-9 indicates that this has indeed been the case. The 21 high-quality growth stocks in this exhibit were selected in 1973, after they had proven that they were growth stocks over the 1962 to 1973 period. All would have made attractive long-term holdings during this time. Exhibit 7-9 shows the percentage drop in the price of each of these high-quality growth stocks over the last four major market declines. Because the stocks did not peak or bottom on the same day, of course, Exhibit 7-9 is an analysis of individual stocks, rather than a market index.

A 40 percent decline is typical for these quality stocks in an adverse market, the type of market that has occurred approximately every four years since the 1940s. Such a decline is quite a shock to any portfolio. Another way to consider the impact of so large a decline is to note that it takes a 67 percent gain to recover from a 40 percent decline.

These stocks were selected after the fact. They provided good total returns over the last decade and were profitable holdings if one had patience and was lucky enough not to concentrate all his buying at the peaks. Nevertheless, these stocks underwent very substantial declines, and they repeated these declines four times in only a 12-year period. Those short-term market moves that the buy-and-hold growth-stock advocates would have us ignore are sharp, severe, and all too frequent.

If, in spite of the dips, these quality growth stocks did provide good returns, they must have more than just recovered from the dips when the market rallied. Indeed, this is the case. Exhibit 7-10 depicts the performance of the same stocks over favorable market periods. We noted that it takes a 67 percent advance to make up for a 40 percent decline suffered in an adverse market. These stocks have provided 67 percent and much more when market conditions were favorable. They advanced 325 percent in the 1962–1965 rally, 184 percent from 1966 to 1969, and 206 percent from 1970 to January of 1973.

These high-quality growth stocks selected at the end of our sample period had a total return (price appreciation and dividends) of 22.2

EXHIBIT 7-9

Bear Market Performance
of Growth—Highest Quality

| | Peak to Trough Percent Declines | | | |
	1962	1966	1970	1973–74
American Express	48.2	30.6	39.4	75.1
American Home Products	50.0	32.2	28.9	46.4
Anheuser-Busch	43.6	16.3	32.2	69.7
Avon Products	49.3	26.3	35.9	86.7
Black & Decker	40.5	34.3	34.2	49.8
Bristol-Myers	41.1	29.2	43.1	58.2
Coca-Cola	35.5	21.1	27.6	70.3
Corning Glass	46.0	28.7	62.8	80.3
Emerson Electric	48.9	26.9	35.4	56.7
IBM	50.9	22.7	43.5	58.8
Intl Flavors & Fragrances	52.2	28.1	36.3	60.6
Johnson & Johnson	43.9	31.1	38.3	45.7
Eastman Kodak	28.0	36.2	33.7	62.4
MMM	53.1	27.4	40.7	51.6
McDonalds	NA	41.7	38.4	72.5
Merck	37.5	17.0	36.2	54.1
Polaroid	66.3	38.3	65.0	90.6
Procter & Gamble	38.0	30.3	48.1	44.2
Sears Roebuck	37.2	42.2	32.0	66.3
Tampax	51.3	32.4	37.1	83.9
Xerox	36.4	53.2	43.6	71.5
AVERAGE	44.9	30.8	39.6	64.5

percent per annum from 1962 to 1972. This return is well above the 9.3 percent return on the S&P 500, indicating why these stocks are now considered "high-quality growth." Their performance of 12.9 percentage points per year over the market average is excellent; any investment manager would be ecstatic if it were his own record. Now,

EXHIBIT 7-10

Bull Market Performance
of Growth—Highest Quality

	Bull Market Percent Gain		
	1962–65	*1966–69*	*1970–73*
American Express	NA	262.5	326.3
American Home Products	105.9	133.7	186.1
Anheuser Busch	279.0	241.0	154.4
Avon Products	347.5	165.9	136.8
Black & Decker	239.5	151.1	234.4
Bristol-Myers	288.4	100.6	54.2
Coca-Cola	162.9	143.4	138.1
Corning Glass	205.0	58.5	117.9
Emerson Electric	205.1	158.9	152.8
IBM	141.2	165.7	108.6
Intl Flavors & Fragrances	668.3	207.9	241.8
Johnson & Johnson	228.5	290.6	257.0
Eastman Kodak	250.2	65.3	163.3
Minnesota Mining & Mfg	110.9	96.3	158.1
McDonalds	NA	878.6	744.1
Merck	309.4	78.3	176.2
Polaroid	758.9	169.9	193.1
Procter & Gamble	46.1	85.7	199.1
Sears Roebuck	161.0	68.3	141.7
Tampax	232.1	155.7	268.5
Xerox	1433.7	175.4	163.4
AVERAGE	324.9	183.5	205.5

however, consider that the 22 percent per annum return from growth stocks consisted of alternate 40 percent declines and 200 percent advances. A little timing of purchases and sales could produce outstanding results compared to the long-term market return or even the return on a group of growth stocks selected by hindsight.

Growth-stock advocates argue that market timing is too difficult and short-term swings in the market are impossible to predict. One is best advised to concentrate on the long-term factors which make growth stocks a superior investment vehicle. To an extent, this viewpoint cannot be disputed; obviously, it is extremely difficult, if not impossible, to predict short-term market swings.

It does appear, however, that investors tend to alternate between euphoria and despair over growth stocks and that paying a little attention to this phenomenon can significantly improve overall returns. Fluctuations in investor sentiment toward growth stocks can be studied in a variety of ways. Our approach is to study indices of various types of growth stocks as compared to the stock market as a whole. Three growth-stock indices will be reviewed: an index of high-quality growth stocks, an index of lesser-quality growth stocks (more speculative than the first group, smaller but still substantial companies), and an index of small growth stocks traded on the American Stock Exchange. These three indices are called High-Quality Growth, Lesser-Quality Growth, and Small Amex Growth respectively. The component companies are shown in Exhibit 7-11.

Exhibit 7-12 (a, b, and c) shows the three indices plotted on a weekly basis from 1968 into 1976. Each chart consists of an index of stock prices, this same index relative to the S&P 500 index, and an advance/decline line. The relative-strength line shows the price performance of the growth stocks relative to the S&P 500 over the previous 25 weeks. A price relative of 1.2, for example, indicates that the growth stocks were 20 percent stronger than the S&P 500 over the 25-week period. This could mean that the growth stocks were up 20 percent while the market was even or that the growth stocks were up 25 percent with the market up 5 percent (actually 4.1667 percent), and so on.

The advance/decline line indicates the breadth of price strength in the growth-stock group, showing the number of stocks advancing, less the number declining, on a given day. For example, if 20 stocks advance and 5 decline on a given day, the advance/decline line would be up 15 for the day. The advance/decline line provides additional insight into the performance of a stock group by showing whether a given increase or decrease in a stock index is broadly based or confined to only a few stocks. A stock price index, for example, will occasionally be moving up while the advance/decline line is flat, implying that a small number of stocks are advancing, perhaps by significant amounts, but that the majority of stocks are even or down slightly.

The three growth-stock groups have consistent patterns of stock

EXHIBIT 7-11

Growth Groups

High Quality

American Express
American Home Products
Anheuser Busch
Avon Products
Black & Decker
Bristol-Myers
Coca-Cola
Corning Glass Works
Eastman Kodak
Emerson Electric
IBM
Intl Flavors & Fragrances
Johnson & Johnson
MMM
McDonalds
Merck
Polaroid
Procter & Gamble
Sears Roebuck
Tampax
Xerox

Small Amex

American Safety Equipment
Coit International
Community Public Service
Corroon & Black
Evans Aristocrat Industries
International Foods
Kaneb Services
Lerner Stores
National Kinney
National Medical Enterprises
Overseas Shipholding
Palomar Financial
Rust Craft Greeting
Ryan Homes
St. Johnsbury Trucking
Service Corp International
Sherwood Medical
    Industries
Standard Products
Synalloy

Lesser Quality

ARA Services
Automatic Data Processing
Digital Equipment
Dr Pepper
Emery Air Freight
Fairchild Camera
Fleetwood Enterprises
Foxboro
General Cinema
Halliburton
Heublein
Hewlett Packard
Holiday Inns
Knight Newspapers
Levitz Furniture
Longs Drug Stores
Marion Labs
Marriott
Masco
Memorex
Motorola
Schlitz Jos Brewing
Simplicity Pattern
Skyline
Standard Brands Paint
Syntex
Teleprompter
Texas Instruments
Texas Oil & Gas
Varian Associates

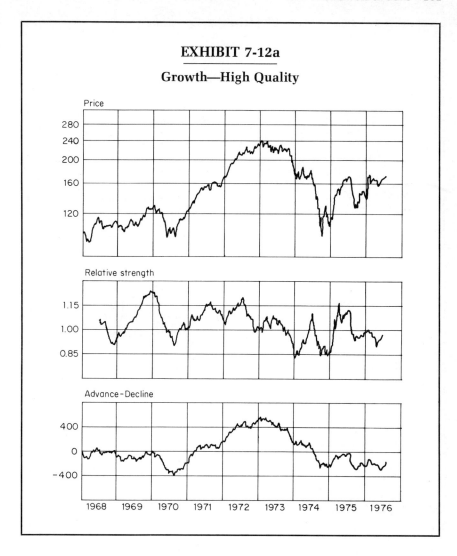

EXHIBIT 7-12a

Growth—High Quality

Price

Relative strength

Advance-Decline

1968 1969 1970 1971 1972 1973 1974 1975 1976

market performance. Consider the High-Quality group (Exhibit 7-12a). After major market declines, this group has a tendency to start slowly, matching or even slightly underperforming the rest of the market for a time. Then as the stock market advance matures, the group keeps advancing when other stock groups have slowed their rate of advance or even begun to decline. It often shows its best relative performance toward the latter stages of the bull market. Finally, after the market as a whole has been declining for some months, the High-Quality Growth

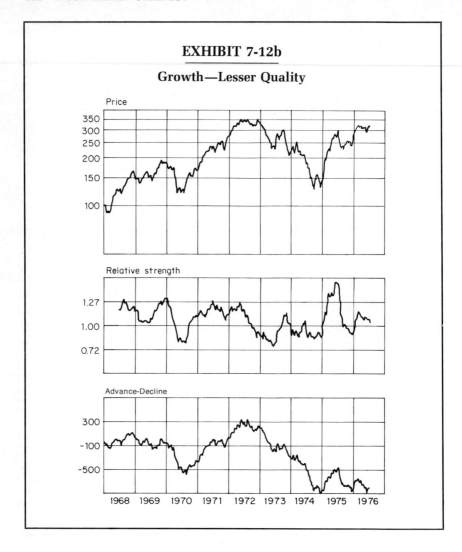

EXHIBIT 7-12b

Growth—Lesser Quality

group tends to collapse suddenly. In this last stage, the stocks often lose 20 to 30 percent in a month or two. In fact, some stock market analysts believe that the decline of the High-Quality Growth group is a favorable sign for the market as a whole, indicating that the bear market is ending.

This pattern can be seen quite clearly in the 1970–1973 period. The High-Quality Growth group held up well through 1969 and into the first half of 1970 as the market was declining. Then it dropped sharply

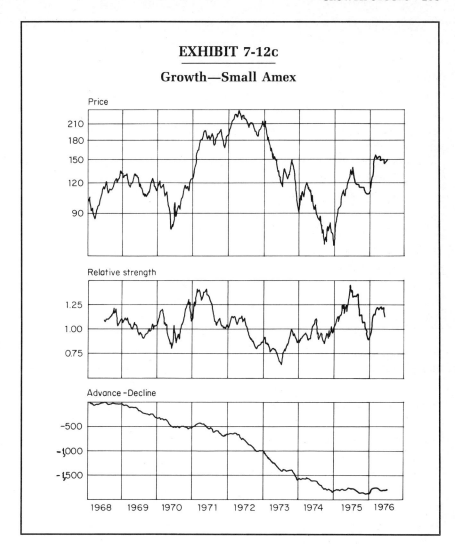

EXHIBIT 7-12c

Growth—Small Amex

in April and May of 1970 at about the same time the popular market indices were making lows. As the market rallied in the last half of 1970, High-Quality Growth equaled the market, as shown by the relative strength line. High-Quality Growth showed more strength in 1971 & 1972, which became stellar years for large growth companies. Relative strength held up quite well for much of 1973 as the overall stock market was declining. Then late in the year, High-Quality Growth became very weak, after almost every other stock had already declined substantially.

Lesser-Quality Growth stocks are growth stocks by any standard, but they are somewhat smaller and do not have quite the institutional following of the premier quality group. Note the considerable similarity to the performance of the High-Quality Growth group. From the market bottom in 1970, these smaller growth stocks advanced rapidly. In the early phase, they were even stronger than the High-Quality group. But Lesser-Quality Growth peaked out earlier. The High-Quality group peaked in January 1973 and actually held up for some months afterward. The Lesser-Quality Growth group peaked much sooner in April and May 1972, and after the peak were quite weak.

The advance/decline line of the Lesser-Quality Growth group also shows the sharp drop in mid-1970, followed by the rapid advance in late 1970 and 1971, the peak in April and May 1972, and the subsequent sharp decline. The drop in the advance/decline line after the peak in the spring of 1972 suggests that this price decline was broadly based and not limited to a few of the Lesser-Quality stocks. They all dropped sharply and most failed to reach new highs in the January 1973 rally.

Exhibit 7-12c shows the performance of a group of American Stock Exchange growth stocks. Many stocks on the American Exchange have been out of favor with investors for several years. However, these are not ordinary American Exchange companies; they have genuine growth credentials. Some have had more than 10 years of consecutive earnings gains. Only their size prevents them from being institutional favorites in the current market environment.

Exhibit 7-12c shows that these stocks rose in an initial flurry after the 1970 market bottom. However, they appear to have peaked in April 1971—about 9 months into the overall market advance, a full year before the peak in Lesser-Quality Growth stocks, and almost 2 years before the peak in High-Quality Growth stocks. The performance of these stocks on an advance/decline basis is particularly striking. Rallies are hardly perceptible. The market bottom in mid-1970 is actually hard to find without looking carefully at the dates on the chart. Long before the market peaked, many of the companies had declined substantially. And whatever rally occurred in this group was not broadly based. The advance/decline line shows that only a few stocks participated to even a small extent in the bull market of 1970 to 1973.

The performance of these growth-stock groups suggest increasing concern or risk-aversion on the part of investors as a bull market cycle progresses. Initially they seem interested in all or many growth stocks.

After a year or less, however, interest in the small growth stocks seems to fade, although investors continue to favor the large but still Lesser-Quality Growth stocks. In fact, the trough-to-peak gains in the Lesser-Quality group are greater than those in the High-Quality group. But Lesser-Quality also tends to peak well in advance of the overall market. The High-Quality Growth stocks continue their advance for the longest period, sometimes even after the majority of stocks are in declines. High-Quality stocks seem to be the last haven for investors who are concerned about the outlook for the market as a whole. But finally, this group also takes a beating, often declining by 40 percent or more. A sharp decline of this magnitude can wipe out most or all of the previous advance, and is especially devastating for an investor unfortunate enough to have bought late in the market advance.

An investor who blindly buys growth stocks for the long term without regard to the market cycle is employing a risky strategy. Better to pay some attention to the performance of stocks to determine investors' current interest in them. If interest is low and you have reason to believe that it will shortly return, you may be looking at a good opportunity. But if prices of your favorite growth stocks are booming, remember that even growth stocks of the highest quality travel a two-way street and can take severe losses. Perhaps waiting until prices drop to more reasonable levels is warranted. Investing in growth stocks should be dependent on market forecasting and an understanding of the dynamics of the particular class of growth stocks as well as on selection of appropriate growth companies.

SELECTING GROWTH STOCKS

There is a great difference between real growth stocks and other stocks. If earnings and dividend growth do turn out to be superior, to exceed investor expectations either in the rate or the duration of growth, the stock will probably provide a superior return over the long term. And even over the short term, a superior growth stock is more likely to attract investor interest within a particular market cycle.

Are there any guidelines for selecting stocks likely to attain above-average earnings growth? Stock market lore is filled with general guidelines, some of which are not operational or definitive, but they are helpful in setting a general framework. After considering these, we will turn our attention to a concept called sustainable growth.

Numerous stock market commentators have offered guidelines to help determine if a company will indeed have earnings and dividend growth to match or exceed investor expectations. One investment firm describes a growth stock as "A share in a progressive, growing company, which is operating in a fertile field of opportunity and benefiting from discernible technological, social, and economic trends, plus able management." The term "progressive" suggests a certain aggressiveness on the part of a company and a willingness to take advantage of new trends and shifts in customer requirements. A "fertile field of opportunity" refers to a product area that is dynamic and changing rapidly, not locked into traditional static patterns. This particular investment firm places considerable emphasis on able management. The assumption is that only the best corporate managers will be able to capitalize on changing trends to make their company grow.

Other growth-stock enthusiasts list related criteria for selecting potential growth companies. An above-average rate of demand growth for a company's products is certainly essential. Actually, a basic definition of growth is a discernible, though manageable, lag between demand and supply. For a company to continue growth at an above-average rate, demand must continue to increase and to exceed supply over a period of years.

Growth-stock advocates also favor companies whose labor costs are a modest proportion of revenues. Companies with high labor costs are more often affected by labor difficulties and inflationary wage increases. Similarly, energy and raw material sources should be considered. A company that is dependent on scarce resources will fall victim to escalating costs. Those in a position to supply these resources—or to produce the capital equipment needed to supply them—are more favorably positioned.

Pricing flexibility too can be a key factor, especially in the current economic environment. Nearly every firm must raise prices from time to time to keep ahead of rising costs. Companies in highly competitive markets will be unable to raise prices and will find their profit margins under pressure, while those that dominate their market can more easily pass increased costs to customers, thereby maintaining profit margins.

Minimal government regulation is another characteristic of growth stocks. A company that must clear every important management decision with a government regulatory body is faced with a considerable impediment to growth. Government regulators can find innumerable reasons to delay plant expansions, to review pricing policies, to study the ramifications of this and that, all slowing the progress of the company. It is not our purpose here to evaluate the wisdom of such government regulation, merely to suggest that the price of regulation is slower growth. Companies subjected to this regulation are less likely to attain above-average growth over the long term and less likely to attract strong investor interest.

In short, growth stocks are companies who, by and large, control their own destiny. A company that is subject to the whims of government regulation or of economic fluctuations or a strong labor union has more difficulty in determining its destiny than other companies free from these constraints. Of course, no company is totally free in the modern business world. Our economy has become too complex, too interdependent for any company to be totally in control of its own future. The skill with which the company adapts to these problems and overcomes them determines its success as a growth company.

SUSTAINABLE GROWTH

The concept of "sustainable growth" combines two additional criteria that are frequently used to identify a growth company: financial condition and profitability. Sustainable growth is a measure of the rate at which a company is reinvesting in itself, that is, the rate at which it can sustain growth from its own financial resources. The concept compares retained earnings (the portion of total earnings not paid out to shareholders as dividends but retained in the firm to finance growth) to total equity. If reinvestment (retained earnings) is large compared to the current size of the firm (total equity)—say, reinvestment is 15 to 20 percent of equity—the company has the potential to grow at an above-average rate in the future. On the other hand, if retained earnings represent only 3 to 5 percent of total equity, the company is simply not reinvesting in itself at a rapid enough rate for investors to expect exceptional growth in the future.

Consider American Telephone, a strong company earning about 9 percent on its equity capital. However, AT&T pays out 65 percent of its earnings as dividends. That is, 65 percent of the 9 percent return on equity goes out to shareholders, and only 35 percent of the 9 percent return, about 3 percent, goes for expansion of the business. Over the long term, earnings per share growth for AT&T probably will not exceed this rate.

Xerox, on the other hand, earns about 21 percent on its equity. After paying out 24 percent of this in dividends, the company still has 16 percent of equity to reinvest each year in the growth of the company. Obviously, Xerox is financially able to sustain a much higher rate of growth than AT&T.

Sustainable growth, or retained return on equity, represents the rate at which a firm is financing its own growth. As long as the company's key financial factors—return on assets, leverage, dividend payout, and so forth—remain unchanged, the company will continue to grow at this rate.

Security analysts interested in why a company is growing and learning more about how it is financing this growth can have a field day with sustainable growth. Exhibit 7-13 breaks sustainable growth into numerous components, all related to the company's income statement and

---

EXHIBIT 7-13

Formulas for Sustainable Growth

Sust. growth = retained return on equity

$$= \frac{\text{(after tax profits} - \text{dividends)}}{\text{equity}}$$

Sust. growth = (earnings retention rate) $\times \dfrac{\text{after tax profits}}{\text{equity}}$

Sust. growth = (earnings retention)

$$\times \left[\frac{(1 - \text{tax rate}) (\text{oper. inc.} - \text{interest} - \text{deprec.}) - \text{pfd. div.}}{\text{equity}} \right]$$

Sust. growth = (earnings retention)

$$\times \left[\frac{(1 - \text{tax rate}) (r \times \text{assets} - i \times \text{debt} - \text{deprec.}) - p \times \text{pfd.}}{\text{equity}} \right]$$

Sust. growth = (earnings retention) $\Big[(1 - \text{tax rate})$

$$\times \left(r + \frac{\text{debt}}{\text{equity}} (r - i) - \frac{\text{deprec.}}{\text{equity}} \right) + \frac{\text{pfd}}{\text{equity}} \times ((1 - \text{tax rate}) \times r - p) \Big]$$

Where: r = operating income/total assets
$\quad\quad\ i$ = average interest rate in long-term debt
$\quad\quad\ p$ = preferred dividend rate

balance sheet. Each formula in Exhibit 7-13 is an equivalent version of sustainable growth, differing only in level of detail. In most cases, however, the very straightforward initial form—sustainable growth rate equals retained earnings (after tax profits less dividends) as a percentage of equity—will suffice.

USING SUSTAINABLE GROWTH

Is a concept as simple as sustainable growth useful in selecting growth stocks? Logically, yes, because companies that reinvest in themselves at high rates should grow faster than companies that fail to reinvest their profits. As a simple test of this hypothesis, the 46 growth companies selected in 1962 by successful mutual funds were analyzed. Specifically, each company's 1962 sustainable growth rate was estimated, based on 1962 financial data. This calculation could have been performed as soon as the company's 1962 financial statements were made public, no doubt early in 1963. The resulting 1962 sustainable growth rates for each company are shown in Exhibit 7-14.

The 1962 sustainable growth rates range from Xerox's 26.9 percent down to Southern Pacific's 1.4 percent. Since company data can be distorted by unusual financial results for a given year, 1962 results alone should not be taken as conclusive evidence of long-term growth prospects. Nevertheless, the results are striking; many of the successful growth stocks of the last 10 years had high sustainable growth rates in 1962: Xerox, Avon, Polaroid, IBM, MMM, and others. On the other hand, many of the stocks that failed to prove themselves as growth stocks had low sustainable growth rates on the basis of 1962 data: Scott Paper, duPont, Grace, AT&T, United Aircraft, and so on.

Sustainable growth is not an infallible measure. Lockheed had a high sustainable growth rate and failed to grow, while Merck, Coca-Cola, and Kodak did far better than their 1962 levels of sustainable growth would suggest. There are many reasons why future growth can differ from realized growth. A complete discussion is beyond our scope here, but some factors can be mentioned briefly. For one thing, a shift in profit margins can have a dramatic effect. In other cases, management policy may change to enhance the rate of sustainable growth. Weyerhaeuser, for example, improved its sustainable growth rate over the last few years by changing established financial policies that were impeding its growth. Weyerhaeuser raised its debt/equity ratio, thereby leveraging itself to a higher return on equity and increased its earnings

EXHIBIT 7-14

1962 Consensus Growth Stocks
Sustainable Growth Rate in 1962

	Sustainable Growth 1962	Realized EPS Growth 1962–72	Return 1962–72
Xerox Corporation	26.9%	27.5%	31.4%
Avon Products	16.1	17.1	26.9
American Greetings	7.8	12.2	25.2
Northwest Airlines	11.4	3.8	25.1
Merck & Company	4.8	15.0	23.8
Coca-Cola Company	5.6	14.0	23.7
Whirlpool Corporation	9.7	9.1	23.5
Polaroid Corporation	13.1	18.7	21.9
Eastman Kodak Company	5.7	14.1	20.9
Burlington Industries	6.8	1.6	16.2
International Business Mach.	13.5	14.6	16.2
ACF Industries	3.3	4.4	16.2
Pepsico	8.3	10.1	16.1
First National Citicorp.	4.3	9.5	15.4
Bristol-Myers Company	13.6	13.3	14.4
Minnesota Mining & Mfg.	10.4	10.2	14.0
International Tel. & Tel.	5.2	12.3	13.4
Pfizer	7.9	8.6	12.6
Coastal States Gas Corp.	26.3	15.0	11.3
Sunbeam Corporation	6.0	1.4	10.2
Ford Motor Company	9.0	4.1	9.8
General Motors Corporation	9.6	−.9	9.8
Rohm & Haas Company	10.7	2.2	8.9

retention rate. The combination nearly doubled Weyerhaeuser's sustainable growth rate.

To an investor, the most important test of sustainable growth is whether it can assist in making better growth-stock selections. The evidence from our admittedly limited sample of 46 stocks selected in

	Sustainable Growth 1962	Realized EPS Growth 1962–72	Return 1962–72
Southern Pacific Company	1.4%	5.6%	8.9%
Exxon Corporation	4.0	5.0	8.8
Royal Dutch Petroleum	5.1	5.3	8.8
Gulf Oil Corporation	5.9	4.6	8.3
Hercules	7.7	5.9	7.7
Reynolds Industries	8.8	6.1	6.7
United Aircraft Corporation	1.5	8.5	6.7
International Nickel	6.0	1.1	6.6
Texaco	7.6	6.1	6.6
Donnelley & Sons	8.2	6.3	5.2
Arkansas Louisiana Gas	7.7	2.4	4.6
Florida Power & Light	5.8	8.1	3.9
Union Carbide Corporation	4.3	0.0	3.8
American Electric Power	4.2	6.3	3.3
American Tel. & Telegraph	3.5	3.8	3.1
Tampa Electric Company	7.6	6.5	3.0
Pitney-Bowes	8.1	2.1	2.4
Virginia Electric & Power	5.6	5.6	.8
W. R. Grace & Company	4.3	−2.4	.2
du Pont	3.5	−3.1	−.2
Addressograph-Multigraph	7.8	−3.8	−1.4
Scott Paper Company	4.2	−2.5	−3.4
Lockheed Aircraft Company	15.7	−13.0	−8.2

1962 by growth mutual funds is favorable. By arbitrarily dividing the sample of 46 stocks into two groups—based on 1962 sustainable growth rates either above or below 10 percent—the resulting performance difference is striking. Of the 46 stocks, only 10 had 1962 sustainable growth rates above 10 percent. These stocks returned an average of 16.2 percent per annum to their shareholders from 1962 to 1972. On the other hand, the 36 stocks with 1962 sustainable growth rates less than 10 percent provided total returns of only 9.2 percent to shareholders in the next 10 years.

This test is based on a very limited sample and should not be construed as a definitive test of sustainable growth as an aid to selecting growth stocks. From the random walk discussion, we know no simple concept can beat the market. But the superior investment performance of the high 1962 sustainable growth stocks does suggest that the concept should be carefully evaluated by growth-stock investors. In short, companies that do reinvest in themselves at high rates have a better opportunity for growth than those that do not.

CONCLUSION

Growth stocks are key investment vehicles for most investors. But there are many misconceptions about the nature and performance of growth stocks:

First, when most investors discuss growth stocks, they mean stocks that *have* grown, not necessarily stocks that *will* grow. Almost all lists of favorite growth stocks are dominated by the successful growth stocks of the recent past. There is absolutely no guarantee that these stocks will continue to grow.

Second, investors often forget that growth stocks, like all other investment vehicles, require two decisions: when to buy and when to sell. For example, holding the growth stocks of 1962—even those stocks that successful institutional investors considered the best growth stocks of that year—for a 10-year period resulted in a rate of return very similar to that of the total market. Indeed, the successful mutual funds outperformed their own 1962 growth holdings, indicating that they engaged in considerable switching over a period of years.

Third, growth stock investing requires a strong sense of market timing; it is definitely not a means of avoiding market judgments, as suggested by many growth stock advocates. Growth stocks are particularly volatile at various phases of the market cycle. Even the highest-quality growth stocks of the past decade—the biggest and the best— have frequently dropped 40 percent in a few months. Lesser-quality growth stocks have been even more volatile, rising more rapidly than their larger counterparts in the early stages of a broad market advance, and dropping more sharply, and much earlier, than the highest-quality group.

This is not to say that growth stocks are less valuable than other stocks. Both financial theory and stock market history attest to their value. Investors should be willing to pay higher P/E ratios as well as accept lower current dividend yields from stocks whose earnings and dividends are expected to grow at an above-average rate in the future. But investors should not expect superior total returns from holding growth stocks unless they are able to select from a wide field those stocks whose earnings will grow more rapidly or for a longer period of time than other investors expect. This is a surprisingly difficult task.

Various criteria have been suggested as aids in selecting growth stocks. These include a progressive management, favorable technological and economic trends, increasing demands for the company's product lines, low labor content, and pricing flexibility. Sustainable growth, the rate at which a company reinvests in itself, the rate it financially sustains its own growth, is a useful quantitative tool.

Notice that we have not suggested that growth companies are from any particular sector of the economy. It is true that in recent years, growth stocks have been predominately from the consumer sector—American Home Products, Coca-Cola, Kodak, Merck, Procter & Gamble—and from the technology or computer areas—Burroughs, IBM, Xerox, and so on. This is only the recent experience. Nearly every major industry in the United States today was at one time a growth area, and the leading companies were considered growth stocks. Railroads had their day in the late 1800s. Autos boomed in the 1920s and 1930s. In the 1950s, it was aluminum and electric utilities. In the early 1960s, airlines had a strong growth period.

There are always growth companies around, but today's success stories are not necessarily the same as yesterday's. The cast changes as time passes. The list sometimes changes relatively slowly. An IBM can remain a growth stock for 30 or 40 years. Something else may lose its growth image after only a year or two. Selecting growth stocks requires some analysis of where the overall economy is going and the companies most likely to benefit from those trends. Growth-stock selection must be forward-looking even though many companies that did well recently are likely to continue in favor—witness the investor interest in Polaroid long after earnings had stopped expanding. Reviewing a list of yesterday's growth stocks can provide considerable insight into today's. But it is only a place to start.

Exhibit 7-15 is a checklist for evaluating whether a candidate company is likely to grow at an above-average rate in the future. It includes most of the key factors mentioned by growth-stock advocates—man-

EXHIBIT 7-15

Growth-Stock Checklist

1. Management skill

   Is the management of the company known for its outstanding professional management ability?

2. Product sales growth

   Are the products of the company growing in unit sales at a high rate? Is this rate of demand growth likely to continue in the future?

3. Low labor content

   Are labor costs a low or moderate proportion of total production costs? Are strikes and labor difficulties likely to interrupt earnings growth?

4. Scarce resources

   Does the company control its own raw material sources? Is it dependent on suppliers for scarce resources likely to increase sharply in price?

5. Product pricing

   Does the company dominate the markets it serves so that it can raise prices when necessary? Or is the company a small factor in its key markets, dependent on others to set the pace?

6. Minimal government regulation

   Is the company free of government regulations, contracts, or antitrust problems?

7. Management control

   Does the company's management control the destiny of the company? Or is the company at the mercy of the economy, bankers, suppliers, competitors, or the government?

8. High sustainable growth

   Can the company finance its own growth at a satisfactory rate? While the satisfactory rate varies from company to company, usually dependent on the growth rate of the markets the company serves, a rule of thumb for large companies is:

$$\frac{\text{Earnings after taxes} - \text{dividends}}{\text{Equity}} \quad \text{well above 0.10 or 10\%}$$

agement skill, unit product growth, and so on, as well as the concept of sustainable growth. Like all checklists, this should be applied with judgment. A diversified list of companies passing these criteria will be interesting candidates for inclusion in an investment portfolio. Of course, their risk characteristics, the market outlook, their current valuation, and their relationship to the current market theme must also be considered.

True growth stocks, shares in companies whose earnings and dividends will grow rapidly in the future, are very likely to be outstanding investments. Traditionally, companies that do grow have provided high rates of return to their patient shareholders. Such stocks are very difficult to find, but are worth the search. Find them. Buy them. But be patient and buy them when they're relatively cheap. Furthermore, don't hesitate to sell them when they're dear, because one day they'll be cheap again. Then you'll have another chance to buy those favorite growth stocks.

EIGHT
Staying in Tune

Every day that the market is open—and even when it is closed—stock prices change. Some are up, some are down, and others drift along, apparently going nowhere. The fluctuations are continuous, never ending, unceasing. It is as if a breeze were blowing across a pond, sometimes from the north, sometimes from the south, sometimes strong, sometimes barely causing a ripple. The water is constantly swirling in one direction and then another. While it may seem for a short time that a trend is developing, soon the wind shifts and the pattern changes.

The winds that affect the stock market are from the social, political, economic, and financial events that affect our daily lives. The stock market is a reflection of the hopes and fears of millions of investors. As individuals are affected by the changing times in which we live, their attitudes toward the stock market are altered. Indeed, the stock market amplifies these events. A new social or political or economic trend which, to the average person, is just a hint of things to come, may be the theme of an entire market move. News that gasoline may be a little hard to obtain is just another annoyance to the average consumer, but it can cause a 50 percent drop in the stock prices of major automobile manufacturers.

The astute investor must be aware of two aspects of this market theme phenomenon. First, there are tremendous profits to be made from properly interpreting the current market theme. If you can be early—not the first, but early—at detecting the current theme and acting on it, you can do very, very well. On the other hand, inability to detect the current market theme can be disastrous. You may end up holding apparently cheap stocks which, because they are out of favor with the current theme, just get cheaper and cheaper. Staying in tune with the market theme is an important element of stock market success.

The second aspect of this phenomenon is even more important. The current theme will end. It may last a few weeks, a few months, maybe even a year or two, but it will pass. It will pass because it really is not true. Whatever the concept that has captured the attention of the market, it will be supported by arguments that seem most rational, most persuasive, most convincing—all tending to make us believe that *this* theme is really true, that this theme will last forever. But it will not. It will end sooner than most people think, and stock market attention will turn to a new theme. So ride the theme while it lasts, knowing that it will end, and prepare to switch to the new theme when it comes along.

All this probably seems confusing and contradictory—jumping onto themes that cannot last just because everyone else thinks they will last. Indeed, some investors find the whole market theme phenomenon so disconcerting that they prefer to ignore it. They just hold onto their stagnant or even fading stocks in hopes that they will return to investment favor. If they wait long enough, these stocks probably will be favored by some new market theme. But it is far less profitable and even dangerous to ignore the market theme, because the stocks they hold tenaciously may be so out of favor with the current theme that they are downright disasters.

It is true, of course, that the stock market is composed of an unending sequence of themes, most of which are so brief that it is impossible to profit from them. While the astute investor is well advised to try to understand even the most brief trend, no one is suggesting that stock market transactions be based on them. They are so brief that their only value is educational, possibly providing a clue to the next major market theme.

Now let's examine some important market themes of recent years, remembering that in each case considerable profits accrued to those investors who participated. On the other hand, those who ignored the theme did so at considerable peril to their financial success. We will also examine the underlying logic of each theme, the basic economic, financial, political, or sociological rationale that supported it. This rationale seemed all-persuasive at the time, as world events and stock price trends confirmed and substantiated the market's theme. But, in the end, the rationale proved false, the theme ended, and the market turned its collective attention to some new problem or opportunity.

THE SHORTAGE THEME

The 1973 theme was shortages and inflation. As 1973 began, the country had been living for some time under a system of wage and price controls intended to curb inflation and restore economic prosperity. This all went under the banner of the Nixon administration's New Economic Policy or NEP, as it was dubbed by the news media. In mid-January 1973, the economy was reaching full operating capacity and concern mounted over union wage demands. The Nixon administration announced Phase IV of its New Economic Policy. Essentially, Phase IV relaxed wage and price controls and attempted to move partway back to a free market system for determining prices and wages.

The stock market's interpretation was that inflation could not be kept in check. The market's interpretation could be seen a week or two after the Phase IV announcement, as most stock prices declined but shortage and inflation stocks rallied. Investors were selling a broad list of stocks—retailers, leisure time, transportation, industrials, and others—and rushing into stocks that benefited from difficult economic times. Gold stocks were strong, since a depreciated dollar means higher gold prices. Suppliers of resources such as copper, aluminum, and steel, and companies that build equipment for electrical power stations moved up. The trend was apparent by the end of January 1973, and continued throughout the year and into 1974.

To be sure, there was some fluctuation about the basic theme. Oil stocks, suppliers of an important resource in short supply, were mixed. International oils tended to fluctuate with the news on oil embargos. Coal stocks were alternately in and out. High-Quality growth stocks—to be discussed shortly—continued strong through much of the year on the grounds that they had the economic muscle to grow in spite of inflation. The astute investor could have noted the major theme by the end of January, adjusted his or her portfolio, and made 1973 a tolerable if not an especially profitable year in the stock market.

The shortage-inflation theme of 1973 was based firmly on the economic trends of the day. It was a very rational, very plausible story. The economy was booming and overheated. Industry was operating at high rates, using almost all available capacity. Raw materials were in short supply. Indeed, these same factors were a problem on a worldwide basis. Inflation was a greater problem in Europe and Japan than here, and, with the oil embargo, no end seemed in sight. It looked from any reasonable viewpoint as though shortages and inflation would be the investment theme for the indefinite future. We now know that the shortages disappeared in the 1974–1975 economic recession. Nevertheless, shortage stocks had a good run in the market. It was a profitable theme for those who perceived it early.

THE ONE-DECISION THEME

The stock market had a different theme in 1972. The 1972 theme had to do with pension funds and large institutional investors—who serve as investment advisors to these pension funds—and a small number of stocks called one-decision, High-Quality growth stocks. The logic was as follows: Large corporate pension funds are the dominant source of new investment in the stock market. It is estimated that corporations put over $10 billion into new equity investments for their pension funds in 1972. Most of the pension fund money is managed by large institutional investors, many of whom are trust departments of large banks already managing other billions in equity accounts. With all this equity money at stake, in-and-out trading is virtually impossible. To an extent, these large institutions are trapped into a policy of buying a stock and putting it away forever. They couldn't sell if they wanted to.

So what do they do? They buy so-called "one-decision" stocks where trading is not required. These stocks just keep growing and growing—so the story goes—overcoming recessions and competition and inflation and leaping tall buildings in a single bound. So what if the price seems a little high at the moment? Over the long haul, earnings growth will pull them through. Anyway, we cannot buy those two-decision cyclical stocks—because we might have to sell them, and we are too big to sell. Similarly, we cannot buy small growth companies because they might have a shortfall in growth, a flat quarter or worse. Then we would have to sell and, again, we are too big to sell. So, we will just buy the growth stocks that will always be in favor, like IBM and Xerox and Disney and Avon.

Skeptics argued that these growth stocks often take sharp dips in bear markets, particularly near the end of severe bear markets and, besides, throughout 1972 they seemed vastly overvalued. The answer was—was, not is—that it won't happen this time because the big bank trust departments will not sell no matter what happens. They will support the price forever. It's the only way for them to invest in these uncertain times.

Despite the obvious fallacies of the one-decision argument, there is no question that it was very profitable while it lasted. These stocks continued to outperform the stock market as a whole from early 1972 until late in 1973. In fact, they were outstanding investment vehicles from the market bottom in the summer of 1970 through late 1973. Three years is a long time for any theme.

Then it happened. The stock market went on to a new theme, and High-Quality growth stocks died. In the previous market declines of 1962, 1966, and 1970, these stocks declined 40 percent or so. Was it so hard to see that history would repeat and the 1972–1973 boom would end in the same type of decline? But few had the foresight to avoid the growth-stock debacle of 1974.

SMALL GROWTH STOCKS

The theme of 1967 and 1968 was especially interesting because of its contrast with the high-quality growth theme of 1972. The opposites were true in 1967 and 1968. That was the era of *small* growth stocks, stocks that could grow and thrive and provide instant rewards to their shareholders because they were small and not subject to the bureaucracy and inflexibility of large companies. This was the era of National Student Marketing, nursing homes, environmental protection companies, franchising Kentucky Fried Chicken and a host of other products and services, Viatron—the computer terminal company that would defeat IBM at $39 a month—and, of course, conglomerates.

In a way, conglomerates best exemplified the lunacy of the stock market at that time. Conglomerates acquired a number of small companies—not those small flexible companies that were growing so fast—but small, slow-growing, cyclical companies which when combined into a large company, had—not bureaucracy and inflexibility—but synergy. Synergy is the ability to make the whole greater than the sum of the parts, presumably through the interaction of all the disparate components into a successful enterprise. Granted, there were some stronger arguments in favor of conglomerates. They could provide strong top management and strong financial resources. But all these were available in those big companies the market despised.

Exhibit 8-1 shows what happened. In 1967 and 1968, small companies soared. The chart shows the ratio of an index of low-priced stocks, mostly small companies, to high-quality stocks. The latter are not the growth stocks that became popular in 1972, but just large companies, the giants of American industry. These small, low-priced stocks outperformed larger companies and the popular market indices by wide

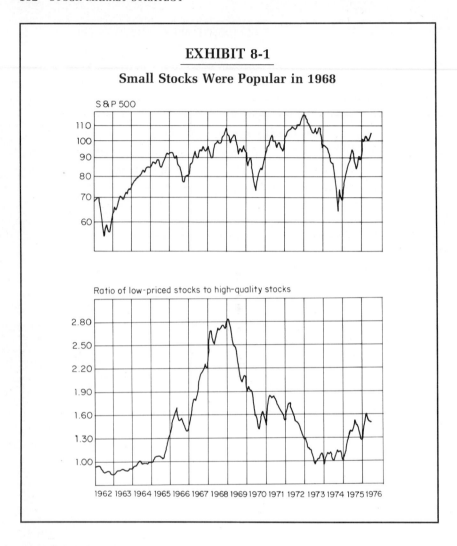

EXHIBIT 8-1

Small Stocks Were Popular in 1968

margins and provided fantastic returns to those stock market investors who detected the trend early.

Exhibit 8-2 shows the performance of a few of the small companies that were market favorites in 1967 and 1968. The exhibit shows the 1966 bear market low for each stock, the high price for 1968–69, and the percentage gain in each stock. Few investors were so fortunate as to buy these stocks at their lows and sell at their highs, but the gains for this type of stock were so extraordinary that even late buyers and early (or late) sellers made handsome profits. Whittaker, a conglomerate that made many acquisitions during this period, was a market leader, rallying nearly 600 percent. Palomar Financial, a small, rapidly growing savings and loan association, went up over 500 percent. Apeco, the former American Photocopy, introduced an office copier. Apparently, investors thought it had the potential to be another Xerox, as the stock price rallied 300 percent. Many others rallied in excess of 100 percent as speculation in small stocks with growth potential was rampant.

This theme, like all the others before and after, ended. It ended in the bear market of 1969–70 and the 1970 economic recession when earnings of many small companies tumbled. The difficult economic environment of 1970 proved that many of these small growth companies were not growth companies after all. In many cases, earnings dropped precipitously, or disappeared altogether. Bankruptcies of previous high fliers such as National Student Marketing and Viatron were com-

EXHIBIT 8-2

Representative Small Growth Stocks 1966–1970

	Low price 1966	*High price 1968–69*	*Percent gain*	*Low price 1970*	*Percent loss*
American Safety Equipment	4¾	18¼	+284.2	4½	−75.3
Apeco	5⅝	22½	+300.0	6	−73.3
Atlas Corp.	2⅝	8¼	+214.3	2⅛	−74.2
Cerro Corp.	29⅛	45¼	+55.4	15⅜	−66.0
Corroon & Black	9⅛	26⅝	+191.8	13¾	−48.4
Evans Aristocrat Ind.	2⅛	10⅝	+400.0	2⅞	−72.9
Gulton Inds.	24⅜	59¼	+143.1	6	−89.9
Lehigh Valley Inds.	7¼	17¼	+137.9	3½	−79.7
Libby McNeil	9⅝	19⅛	+98.7	5	−73.9
Palomar Finl	1¾	10¾	+514.3	4½	−58.1
Publicker	5⅞	19¼	+227.7	4⅝	−76.0
Rust Craft	9¼	19¼	+108.1	9¼	−52.0
St. Johnsbury Trucking	8⅞	22⅜	+152.1	8	−64.3
Standard Prods.	8⅛	15	+84.6	9⅛	−39.2
Synalloy	8¾	23⅛	+164.3	4⅛	−82.2
Welbuilt	2⅛	11⅝	+447.1	3	−74.2
Whittaker	6⅝	45⅞	+592.5	5	−89.1

mon. Their stock prices fell sharply, in many cases far more than would seem justified by the earnings decline. Exhibit 8-2 also shows the 1969–70 bear market performance of representative favorites from the 1967–68 small stock theme. Many declined 60 or 70 percent, and some stocks dropped nearly 90 percent. The conglomerate Whittaker, which rallied from $6 and a fraction to $45, dropped all the way back to $5. Apeco's 300 percent gain evaporated as the stock bottomed a shade above its previous low. Palomar bottomed in 1970 at more than double its price in 1966, small consolation to those who bought near the top and took a 58 percent loss. In fact, most of the stocks in Exhibit 8-2— and these are representative of the period, not the worst examples by any means—bottomed in 1970 about where they were in 1966, and many have continued to decline since.

The small stock theme ended in the bear market of 1969–1970. This was apparent from Exhibit 8-1, which showed the performance of the low-priced index relative to the high-quality stock index. This does not mean that the trend cannot reverse itself. But to date it has not, and investors who purchased small growth stocks almost anytime from late 1968 to now have been disappointed.

No matter how significant the earnings growth or how undervalued the stock price, by and large, the stock price performance has been poor. When a market theme is over and done, subsequent investment performance can be very poor, in spite of growth and undervaluation.

EARLIER THEMES

Stock market themes come and go. They have come and gone as far back as recorded stock market history. While the examples here are fairly recent, earlier themes might equally be reviewed. In the early 1960s, electronics was a great concept. The space race was on and almost any stock with a scientific or electronics buzzword in its name was almost certain to be a big winner. Most of these collapsed in the 1962 bear market.

In the 1950s, aluminum and utility stocks were the theme stocks. Apparently, war-induced shortages in basic materials and energy were still being worked off. By the early 1960s, at the peak of this theme, leading aluminum companies and the electric utilities with the better growth records sold at P/Es associated with premier growth stocks. Alcoa reached a price of over $50 in 1961, making its P/E over 40. Texas Utilities reached a price of $28 in 1961, selling at a P/E of nearly 35. For the balance of the 1960s, interest in these groups faded. By 1974, Alcoa was selling at only $35 with a P/E of 10, and Texas Utilities had faded to $16. Both remain strong companies, vital components of the American economy. But the market had lost interest. Their theme had ended.

Railroads were popular in the stock market for many decades dating back to the 1800s. The last strong period for railroad stocks ended in the late 1940s. Railroads were, of course, vital to the war effort. But after the war, as air transportation gained and oil replaced coal, one of the chief railroad cargoes, railroad stocks went into a long decline.

Earlier in the twentieth century, General Motors and Bethlehem Steel were considered outstanding growth stocks. According to McNeel[1], Bethlehem Steel went from below $50 to $700 in the war boom of 1915 and 1916 and General Motors went from $106 to over $400 in 1918 and 1919. The Wall Street research reports that sparked these booms are no longer readily available—or at least I did not think them worth tracking down—but one can imagine the theme from the environment. Probably the boom in Bethlehem Steel in 1915–16 was due to war-induced steel shortages. Bethlehem Steel was a major steel supplier and was the recipient of investor concern that the iron and steel shortage induced by the war would be very significant and long lasting. General Motors, on the other hand, did well after the war ended. No doubt GM's stock price boomed because investors expected consumer demand, which had been building during the war, to result in a rush of automobile buying.

Circumstances change. Bethlehem Steel benefited from wartime shortages, a war that in 1915 and 1916 probably looked as though it might last forever. But the war ended, and consumer products returned to favor. So General Motors replaced Bethlehem Steel as a market favorite, and the market theme moved on to a new concept.

THEMES AND CORPORATE EARNINGS

These examples have illustrated the general characteristics of stock market themes. Themes are powerful forces in the stock market. A theme appears, dominates the stock market scene for a while, and fades, only to be replaced by another theme. Stock market themes always end. Though the arguments to support the current theme are most rational and persuasive, though the stocks supported by this

---

[1]R. W. McNeel, *Beating the Stock Market*, Duffield and Company, New York City 1927, p. 80.

theme continue to go up and up, it will end. Predicting when it will end may be difficult or impossible, but it will end. The astute investor must be aware that the current theme's days are numbered, that it is not some new truth destined to dominate investing forever. Take advantage while it lasts, and be prepared to stay in tune by switching to the new theme when the time comes.

Stock market themes are always related to some specific factor, usually to the social, economic, political, and financial environment in which we find ourselves. The 1973 boom in inflation and shortage stocks was a classic example of the economic side at work. The 1972 boom in quality growth stocks was in part economic—these stocks were considered able to grow in spite of inflation—and in part financial—the importance of large bank-managed pension funds in the stock market. Similarly, the booms in Bethlehem Steel and General Motors were closely related to the Great War and therefore might be considered political as well as economic.

An important characteristic of stock market themes is that they are tied to investors' expectations of future corporate earnings. High-Quality growth stocks were favored in 1972 because investors thought their earnings would grow forever, in spite of economic uncertainties. Inflation and shortage stocks did well in 1973 because investors thought that these companies would finally show earnings growth. Paper stocks had been relatively stagnant for years, as had their earnings; but the paper shortage of 1973 led investors to believe that these companies would finally see paper demand exceed supply and earnings growth. Bethlehem Steel went up in 1915 because the war-induced steel shortage implied good earnings for Bethlehem Steel. By the same token, General Motors was popular with investors after the war because pent-up consumer demand was expected to result in growth in GM's earnings. Small growth stocks were popular in 1967 and 1968 because investors felt that small companies were best suited in that era to show rapid earnings growth. In summary, stock market themes usually pursue hoped-for earnings growth. The theme lasts no longer than the earnings potential. In the end, if earnings do not fulfill expectations, the theme will end, and prices of stocks related to the fading theme will likely fall.

The relationship between stock market themes and earnings performance also suggests the continued importance of growth stocks. Companies with the ability to continue earnings growth, to compound earnings gains year after year are much more likely to receive renewed

attention from investors. A growth-stock theme is much more likely to
return than another, less earnings-oriented theme. In our analysis of
growth stocks, we showed how growth stocks fall from favor toward
the end of each bear market cycle, only to return when the stock market
itself recovers. This happened in 1974 and 1970 and 1966 and 1962 and
many times prior to that.

The relationship between the market theme and earnings growth, or
more specifically, investor expectations of earnings growth, also suggests a close tie-in between the business cycle and relative stock market
performance. We already know the business cycle has a strong impact
on the overall stock market. How does the business cycle affect how
one stock group does versus another? It is well known that various
economic sectors lead and lag the overall economic or business cycle.
For example, housing tends to be a leading economic sector. Exhibit 8-
3 shows housing permits in relation to the economic or business cycle.
Housing starts often trough early in recessions and begin to move up
while the overall economy is still stagnant. Housing starts are often
booming by the time the overall economy starts to move ahead. But

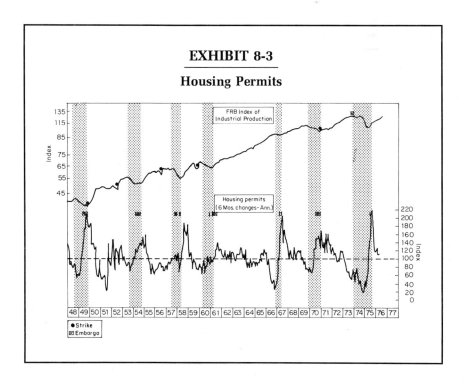

EXHIBIT 8-3

Housing Permits

housing usually turns down in the midst of the overall economic advance, peaking many months in advance of the peak in the general economy.

Companies whose earnings are closely tied to the housing area of the economy should be expected to show significant earnings gains early in the economic cycle, and their stock prices should perform well early in the economic recovery (which is usually a strong period for the overall stock market). In addition, expect to hear all sorts of analyses explaining why these housing stocks have become the new growth stocks. You will hear about chronic housing shortages that will finally be resolved through a big building boom. All this is intended to justify the run-up in housing stocks associated with their relative earnings gains and to sustain this market interest by suggesting that this is not a cyclical, but a growth phenomenon.

Unfortunately, the tie-in between the business cycle and economic sector stock performance relative to the market is imperfect. On occasion, stock prices perform in the supposedly proper order, the sequence in which the business cycle affects various economic sectors. On this basis, housing should be strong early along with the more defensive consumer-nondurables sector. Later, consumer-durables should receive attention. Then, late in the economic expansion, basic materials are likely to be favored as the economy begins to overheat and shortages and inflation become the new theme. However, this neat pattern does not apply consistently. Housing sometimes performs on schedule, but it can be much stronger or much weaker than this simple approach would suggest. Other economic sectors are equally inconsistent. Probably one of the best cases can be made for utilities showing good relative performance at market bottoms. This is more of a defensive strategy.

Consequently, the best application of economic analysis within a business cycle is to determine the economic areas with the best long-run growth potential, the most fertile areas for finding growth stocks. The growth-stock cycle within an overall market cycle is much more predictable, has much higher odds of success, than betting on a particular economic sector to perform on schedule.

At the same time, care must be taken to draw growth stocks from diverse economic sectors. Since the sectors do underperform and outperform the stock market as a whole in what sometimes appears to be a haphazard manner—or a manner that can be explained only by hindsight—overconcentration in one economic sector can be risky. A better approach is to hold a list of growth stocks diversified by economic sector with perhaps some emphasis on the sectors expected to do best at the current phase of the business cycle.

CONCLUSION

To summarize, the market is dominated by themes that are reflected in the relative movements of stock prices. These themes are related to the social, economic, political, and financial characteristics of the times. And these factors are interpreted by the stock market as affecting the earnings and growth potential of various companies, some favorably and some unfavorably.

The fact that they are interpreted as affecting earnings is of assistance to investors because it provides a clue to their successful application. It implies, for example, that normal developments in the business cycle—housing, capital spending, and so on—may be amplified by the market as new themes. An astute investor will expect these developments and capitalize on them.

This association with relative earnings also illustrates the importance of growth stocks. While the degree of emphasis may vary from market cycle to market cycle, history indicates that these stocks are more likely than others to become a new theme. At some point in the economic cycle, frequently near the end of the advance, these stocks will be perceived as having strong relative earnings and will become a new, or should we say renewed, theme.

The importance of relative earnings in establishing and maintaining themes illustrates one of the roles of fundamental security analysis to ferret out those companies likely to show strong relative earnings. At the same time, the fundamental analyst must remember that the association between relative earnings and the stock market theme is imperfect. The stock that seems so undervalued with such great potential for earnings growth just may not be consistent with the current theme of the stock market. Even fundamental security analysis must stay in tune with the market.

Finally, the point that the current stock market theme will not last must be stressed. New themes appear, dominate the market for a while, and then end. They always have. The astute investor must maintain a degree of cynicism that will enable him to play the current game, to take advantage of the current theme. But he must know from the beginning that it will not last. The time will come when the theme is over, a new game has begun, and investments must be adjusted accordingly.

The reason that the current theme, whether it is inflation or shortages or large growth stocks or small growth stocks or whatever, will not last is that the precept on which the theme is based is simply not true. It may be supported by strong arguments and may seem true, but it isn't. The world is not suddenly so different that some new investment theme can be applied now and forever. The only reason that we think so is that our judgment is so fallible and our memory so short that we cannot discern the present trend as really something seen many times before.

DETECTING NEW THEMES

How can you determine that a new theme is about to begin? Frankly, it is extremely difficult, and investors who concentrate only on themes are likely to be whipsawed back and forth. They will probably generate far more brokerage commissions than they will investment profits. About the only guidelines that can be suggested for detecting new themes are (1) stay in touch with what other investors are thinking and (2) keep an eye on technical analysis. Essentially, this is saying that one stays in tune with the market theme by staying in tune with other investors' thoughts. If other investors are worried about inflation, that worry will be reflected in their investment transactions and in stock prices. If they see an opportunity in energy stocks, energy stocks will start to move. They will talk about energy, write about energy, and technical experts will begin to see favorable activities in energy stocks.

You must do a little more than stay in tune with other investors and transactions in the stock market. To effectively utilize the new market theme, you must see a pattern of events and of interest unfolding *before* other investors. They will still be seeing isolated events, individual news items, and interest in single stocks or a few groups of companies. You must put the jigsaw together before they do.

This is no mean feat since the stock market is notoriously early at anticipating coming trends. The stock market sees recessions while public opinion is still concerned about boom and inflation. It sees economic recoveries while newspaper headlines warn only of rising unemployment and business failures. The market sees surpluses while business purchasing agents are busy ordering extra inventories to avoid shortages. If you can see the new trends of investor thinking early, anticipate what they will be worrying about next—not now, but next—and read an overall pattern into isolated changes in stock prices of companies and groups, you can stay ahead of the market theme. It is a very difficult task.

Nevertheless, themes are important to all investors. Selecting stocks consistent with the current market theme can be an important clue toward obtaining superior investment returns. Since interpreting the market theme, both its start and its conclusion, is extremely difficult, theme stocks probably have more risk and more opportunity for return than stocks selected by other techniques. Theme stocks can and should be used in any portfolio, particularly any aggressive portfolio. But theme stocks should not be the sole approach to stock selection. The danger of investor attention switching to a new theme just after your portfolio gets positioned for the old theme is simply too great. Use a few theme stocks, but also consider value and longer-term growth potential.

NINE

Stock Market Strategy

How do we put it all together—the conflicting theories of students of the market, the challenge of the random walk, the frightening implications of risk, the opportunities of return, the difficult task of recognizing bull and bear markets, and the even more difficult task of acting soundly during them, the potential from owning growth stocks at the right time and not owning them at others, and the vagaries and deceptions of staying in tune—how do we put it all together into a sound stock market strategy?

The first step in developing a strategy for the stock market is to review the principle behind the random walk theory of stock prices. The random walk theory is helpful in developing realistic expectations about the returns from owning common stocks. The stock market is highly competitive, and that competition assures that stock prices are a reasonably fair representation of underlying value. Consequently, the opportunities for finding potential winners as yet undiscovered by other investors are very limited. One cannot expect easy successes.

The implication is that most investors, and worse, most professional investment managers, are wasting their time on the wrong problem. They are perennially seeking great individual stocks when, in fact, such opportunities are few and far between. Since success at selecting individual stock winners is so difficult, investors need to devote more effort to the tasks that can really do them some good—risk evaluation and determining the overall investment outlook. They should make stock selection the third and last step in the overall decision process. Stock selection is important. It deserves third, not prime, priority.

Have modest expectations about the returns you might earn in the

193

stock market. If you are able to earn a small amount more than the averages, 3, 2, or even 1 percent per annum better, consider yourself amply rewarded. If you go for much more than this, you must be very, very lucky, or you must take exorbitant risk which in the end will be disastrous.

RISK

Many have taken unwarranted risks. In the bull market that ended in 1968, a number of so-called "gunslingers" fresh out of Harvard Business School masterminded small investments into great fortunes. These bright chaps thought that their success came from their own brilliance. They saw a world of opportunity when their depression-trained predecessors saw only risk. They despised preservation of capital and thought only of further successes, of more growth in capital. In reality, they achieved their apparent success because they took more risk during a period when the market looked kindly on risk, as it does from time to time. But in the bear market of 1969 and 1970, risk acted like risk so often does, and the paper fortunes melted away.

By modest expectations, we are referring to expectations of return relative to the stock market averages. The return to be expected from the stock market as a whole, just from owning common stocks, is quite substantial relative to alternatives. Over time, the market has paid a premium to those willing to bear the risks of owning equities. Historically, returns to owners of common stocks have been something on the order of 7 percentage points per annum over the so-called "risk-free" rate. The risk-free rate refers to returns earned by investors who take no risks, or more realistically, minimum risks, such as available in Treasury bills. Seven percent per annum compounded over many years results in very significant increments to wealth.

Of course, this 7 percent premium to owners of common stocks has not been a constant, year-in, year-out phenomenon. What we mean by willingness to bear the risk of common stocks is willingness to see your returns come in wide-ranging fits and starts; up substantially in one year, and down disastrously in another, with no predictable pattern other than wide fluctuations. Many investors simply cannot afford to bear this kind of risk. That is a question that needs to be faced squarely. Just how much risk can you bear, how much can you afford? There are some very rough guidelines to help here. Young people with relatively little wealth and years of good salary ahead can obviously incur more risk in the hope of extra returns than retired people totally dependent on their wealth for income. Similarly, a pension fund of a small rapidly growing company with relatively young employees can probably be more aggressive than a staid giant of industry with many retirees dependent on its pension fund.

Financial status, as important as it is, is not the whole question. The psychological aspects of risk are equally important. Investors who cannot sleep nights worrying about investments, who live in fear that friends, spouse, or boss will criticize their holdings and laugh at their losses, have excellent reasons for staying out of the market, or at least participating in the market in a modest, lower-risk manner.

Ultimately, each of us must individually study the implications of risk. Take another look at those tables and charts in Chapter Four. Decide how much loss you can tolerate. What would you do if your losses mounted to 20 percent or 30 percent or 40 percent? This is an intensely personal decision. Be especially careful about this decision and don't get caught up in the successes of yourself or others. Too many investors enter the stock market based on hearsay success stories or a rosy sales pitch. They should pay more attention to the very significant risks. To put it another way, many investors take more risk than they should. That can be a very expensive mistake.

Perhaps the best approach is to decide on the maximum risk level that you find tolerable using the risk scale proposed in Chapter Four. Suppose you decide that a risk level of 0.7 (equivalent to 70 percent of your investable assets in the stock market) is about the maximum you can tolerate. Your decision within this range will depend upon your market outlook. You will be close to 70 percent in the stock market when you are very optimistic about the stock market outlook. You will have a much smaller portion, perhaps nothing, in the market if you are pessimistic about the market outlook.

In selecting individual investments, decide in advance how they impact the overall risk of your portfolio. Own a diversified portfolio and regularly calculate the value-weighted average risk. Is it where you want it to be? Too little risk can be just as expensive a mistake as too much risk, so keep up to date on this parameter. Never buy or sell anything in your portfolio until you have considered the risk impact of this decision.

MARKET TIMING

Next, consider the timing of your investments. For many years the market has been going through a bull-bear cycle lasting on the order of

4 years. Not exactly 4 years in the sense of a cycle from physics or electronics. The stock market is far more complex than alternating current. Rather, we are considering a growing optimism on the part of investors which, with fits and starts, lasts on the order of 2 or 2½ years, followed by a more rapid drop of a year or longer. This rapid drop is accompanied by, indeed caused by, growing pessimism on the part of investors.

Where are we in any particular market cycle? If the answer is, early in the advance, great! That probably means the market has recently been to very low levels and is in the early stages of recovery. Economic pessimism, recently rampant, is now giving way to a growing optimism. Corporate profits show signs of turning around and interest rates have probably dropped to levels that a year or two earlier seemed likely never to be seen again. The Federal Reserve is probably espousing a blatantly expansive policy, trying to get the economy moving ahead and vowing that this time it will not allow the mistake of overstimulation which last time around led to excessive inflation. As a result, the market is probably doing rather well, undergoing a broadly based advance with many stocks participating.

If this is the case, the time is likely to be very favorable for a move into the market. Not that any such move can be made with certainty, and not that the market is immune to setbacks even at this stage. It only means that the odds are unusually favorable. If you are going to be in the stock market at all, this is the time.

MARKET PEAKS

However, if the market has far advanced from this stage and seems more like it is approaching the end of the bull market phase, the opposite tactic is warranted. Start getting out of the stock market. Wait on the sidelines in Treasury bills or commercial paper or some safe, high-yield liquid asset. Be prepared to wait for a year or 2 years or whatever it takes to wipe out investor optimism. If the stock market is really nearing the end of a bull market phase, it will not be likely to go through a very brief, but sharp decline and then start back up. This is possible, but not likely. More probably a protracted decline is about to begin. Thus, the best strategy will be to sit on the sidelines far longer than most investors think wise, certainly far longer than the broad consensus of investors think wise.

Keep in mind that the stock market got to its current high level because the vast majority of investors are optimistic. They have bid prices up because they see a rosy outlook. If you sell (or being out of the market, stay out), they are going to think you daft. If you don't see that the current economic boom can last forever, that this time things are different and growth can continue longer, that high interest rates and tight money and inflation will not be the problem this time that they have in past economic booms, if you believe that all this can only lead to economic slowdown and a market collapse—do not expect to win friends on Wall Street. Quietly sell and go sit on the bench until the conditions for the stock market game become more favorable. Be prepared to wait a long time.

BEFORE THE PEAK

There are two phases of the market cycle where the decisions are even tougher. One is when the bull market is in the second or third quarter and the game is moving toward the end but is not over. Much of the advance has already taken place, but not all of it. Probably only a few stocks are continuing to advance.

What to do here? There is no easy answer, but one approach is to keep most of your assets out of the market. Make your limited commitments to the High-Quality growth area—no doubt already beginning to look overvalued—which usually has the most staying power in the latter stages of a bull market. Be especially careful to avoid apparently undervalued situations. These are stocks that have not as yet gained favor in this bull market and are consequently selling at discount P/E ratios. In the latter stage of a bull market, investor confidence wanes and becomes restricted to a handful of the strongest stocks, the stocks with the most going for them in the current environment. It is not the time to expect interest to revive in stocks that have previously been ignored.

Similarly, be wary of small-growth stocks that achieved high multiples early in the stock market advance, but now have dropped down to more reasonable levels. These are likely to be in the early stages of their own bear market, again losing favor as interest shifts to the safer higher-quality issues. They may have one more rally to their old highs or even better. But the odds are against them for the remainder of this cycle.

WHERE'S THE BOTTOM

The most difficult decision is toward the end of bear markets. The bear market has unfolded as investors have become more pessimistic. It may even reach a panic selling phase where stocks are sold at ridiculously low levels because there are no buyers, at least no buyers at reasonable price levels. At this point, economic conditions are likely poor and deteriorating, monetary policy is tight, and there is no end to the decline in sight. Everyone is pessimistic. How do you possibly know when to buy in this environment, especially since the consensus of knowledgeable investors is that anyone who buys now is daft, as daft as the chap who sold in the midst of the bull market?

Somewhere in here is the optimal time to buy. Stock prices are lowest and provide the greatest opportunity for advance. The prices are the lowest and the potential returns the greatest because investors perceive the risks to be the highest. High risk means high potential return, but high risk also means the most difficult decisions. Somewhere in here, when the market is collapsing and the economic outlook is bad and you know prices can go lower because there is no way to forecast how far pessimism will run, how far prices will be beaten down, somewhere in here is the best time to buy.

One clue is that the economic upturn should be barely visible on the horizon and the Federal Reserve should be moving toward an expansive policy to get the economy moving ahead. These are only clues, no hard and fast guidelines to certain success. Wait until you think everyone else has panicked enough, until you can barely see the makings of an economic upturn, and then slowly and carefully start to buy. Start to buy knowing you are going to be wrong in the short term—the market may fall farther tomorrow and the next day. It may take quite a time for this decision to be vindicated. If history is any guide, you will be getting some real bargains.

The market-timing checklists in Chapter Five can be of assistance here. Run through each of the items. Do they indicate that a market peak is approaching, or a market bottom? If neither seems close, the question is greatly simplified. It should be easy to determine whether a bull or bear market is in progress. If the market bottomed a year or so ago during a recession and has been in a general advance since, then a bull market is probably in progress. Keep an eye on the peak indicators and be prepared to sell. On the other hand, if the market is several months into a decline and economic conditions are deteriorating, watch the bottom indicators for a buying opportunity. Don't force it. Be patient, but be ready.

STOCK SELECTION METHODS

Suppose it is time to do some buying, time to increase the risk exposure of your portfolio so you can more fully participate in a stock market advance. What stocks should you buy? There are literally thousands of choices, nearly 2,000 stocks on the New York Stock Exchange alone. How does one decide which stocks to own?

Notice the question is stated in the plural—which *stocks* to own. Trying to pick the best stock is a hopeless task. Many have tried, continue to try, and always fail. The objective should be to select a diversified portfolio of stocks that will fully participate in the market advance. If the market is rising and your stocks are rising, you are earning a profit on your investments. Do not be overly concerned if your portfolio is not the best performer around, if others are doing a bit better. A good return is objective enough. Greed can lead to bad investment decisions, increased turnover and transaction costs, and perhaps undue risk.

The three major stock selection techniques—value, growth, and staying in tune—have all been reviewed. Ideally, we want an undervalued stock with great long-term earnings growth potential in a field currently favored by the market theme. For reasons that have been elaborated, the ideal stock is very difficult to find. Consequently, in order to participate in the rising market and earn a premium return over the risk-free rate, compromises in stock selection must be made. You will have to settle for a few growth stocks that are only fairly valued, not dirt cheap. Your undervalued growth stocks may not be the subject of the current theme. Your theme stocks may have to be a bit overvalued. And so forth.

It is also advisable to own stocks selected from a diversity of criteria—some theme stocks, some growth stocks, some undervalued stocks, and various combinations. You never know when one characteristic or another will become the subject of a new theme. Growth or value can themselves be the subject of their own themes, as has been illustrated. Owning stocks from several different areas provide diversification, which makes it less likely your portfolio will fail to at least partially participate if a new area suddenly attracts the attention of other investors. Of course, it also means some of your holdings will be left behind if the theme shifts. Overall portfolio participation in the rising market trend is the objective, not having every single stock a big winner.

PHASES OF THE MARKET CYCLE

Selection of appropriate stocks must be made in the context of the stock market cycle we have just discussed. As such, it is helpful to think of the advancing or bull market phase of the cycle in the football game analogy of four quarters or four equal time periods. During the first-time quarter of the bull market, most stocks advance sharply as they come off the depressed prices of the bear market, and the advance in the overall market averages is the best, often as much as 50 percent of the gain the bull market will ultimately attain. This rapid advance is funded by a reinvestment wave of broad buying. Cash reserves from the bear market are rushed into the market as investors realize the new bull market has begun.

The second quarter is also very favorable. Again the market averages advance more than another 25 percent of the ultimate overall gain of the cycle, but stock selection becomes more difficult. Investors have usually lost interest in many stocks and have begun to concentrate on a smaller number that have something special going for them. Perhaps they are emerging growth favorites.

By the third quarter, the stock market game is getting much tougher. The overall gain will likely be less than 25 percent of the overall advance, and a restricted number of stocks will be rising. By the fourth quarter, things are really tough. Most of the overall advance has already occurred, so if we get another 15 to 20 percent we should feel very fortunate. Stock selection is extremely difficult, as only the highest-quality growth stocks and a few other stocks that benefit from the more difficult economic times are continuing to advance. At this stage, most investors do not realize the bull market is virtually over. They are hoping all those low P/E stocks will catch up with the current high P/E market favorites. But they won't. Rather, the high P/E favorites are on their last legs and about to fall.

These four quarters of market advance have deliberately been defined in a very loose manner. There are no precise definitions, no exact measures, no certainty that the market is currently in any particular quarter. The problem is made more difficult by the fact that the market is swinging up and down at all times during this generally bullish period. Drops of 100 or 150 points on the Dow Jones Industrial Average occur frequently during bull markets. In spite of this imprecision in the definition of the market quarters, it is a convenient way to express stock selection strategy. In application, the investor can usually make a rough guess at where he is, have a reasonable idea of what to expect next and how he should be adjusting his portfolio holdings to take advantage of the outlook.

STOCK SELECTION AND THE MARKET CYCLE

Keep in mind that the overall performance of the stock market is the major determinant of whether a portfolio is up or down. In this context, performance relative to the market is far less important. Any reasonably diversified portfolio is going to act very much like the major stock market averages, the Dow Jones Industrial Average or the S&P 500 stock averages or whatever. If the averages are up substantially, most diversified portfolios will be up as well. If the averages are down substantially, most diversified portfolios will suffer substantial losses. For the vast majority of diversified portfolios, the amount of relative performance, the amount that they exceed or drop behind the stock market, is almost unimportant.

The major objective of stock market investing is to participate as fully as possible in advancing markets and to avoid the declining markets as much as possible. If you think you are in a bull market, the question then is what types of stocks are most likely to participate fully in the market upswing. What types of stocks have the best chances of seeing their prices bid up as investor confidence returns in the bull market? The answer is, the stocks most likely to show earnings growth. Earnings growth attracts investor interest in virtually every market cycle. It must be earnings growth that investors can convince themselves will continue into the future. While a transitory earnings gain may attract attention for a short time, investors will eventually see the end and move on to other concepts. In short, it must be earnings growth that investors can translate into expectations of even more earnings growth in the future, thereby justifying a higher and higher stock price as the bull market unfolds.

This view argues for an essentially growth-stock approach to bull market investing. Critics will attack this growth-stock approach on several grounds. First, the list of growth stocks changes over time. Hindsight is an imperfect guide to selecting the growth stocks of tomorrow. Growth-stock investing is not a shortcut to investment success that eliminates economic forecasting and security analysis, as some critics will suggest. We want tomorrow's growth stocks, not yesterday's.

Second, growth stocks typically take a terrible beating near the end of bear markets. They are often the last stocks sold as investors become more defensive. But they are sold, and the sharp price declines at the end of bear markets are fresh in investors' minds as the new bull market begins. These sharp losses lead to "growth is dead" discussions by market commentators just when growth stocks are most attractively priced. Indeed, the "growth is dead" concept is necessary to justify the lower prices growth stocks are now selling at in the stock market. The "growth is dead" theme at market bottoms is merely providing the opportunity for price advances as the bull market unfolds.

Third, competing stock selection philosophies abound. One example is undervalued stocks, the Ben Graham approach, as we have seen. At major market bottoms, many stocks are very cheap. Virtually everything is undervalued and most of these stocks are attractive. The problem is that a few months into the bull market these cheap stocks are no longer cheap, especially once interest rates start rising to compete against dividend yields. Undervalued stocks can do well early in bull markets and may even perform throughout the cycle. The problem is that the odds are not as good that they will fully participate as the odds for growth stocks. The euphoria and greed that drive prices up late in bull market cycles is more likely to favor a strong, growing company than a dull stock that is no longer depressed.

STOCK SELECTION IN THE FIRST QUARTER

The first quarter of the bull market advance is a very pleasant experience. Almost everything advances as most stocks rebound from the excessively depressed levels of the bear market. To take a guess at what might do best in this period, at what might be the market theme, try high-risk stocks. Risky stocks are probably the most battered from the bear market, as they had the highest probability of actually going bankrupt. In the pessimism and panic of a bear market, it doesn't take much financial uncertainty to send investors fleeing and stock prices to very low levels. As liquidity returns to the economic system, the threat of bankruptcy abates, and these stocks return to more normal levels.

The market theme at this stage is likely to be risk. High-risk stocks can do well for a while.

What about growth stocks? Some of the smaller ones may actually be included in this risk theme. Investors fled the small growth stocks, fearing their financial security in a difficult economic climate, among other things. But as confidence returns, these smaller growth stocks can do very well.

The High-Quality growth stocks often turn in a mediocre performance during the first quarter, perhaps gaining in line with the stock market averages. Nothing spectacular. Solid performance, but not first place, nothing to attract the headlines as yet. Still, a solid gain in value in these highest-quality stocks is not to be scoffed at.

One of the characteristics of major market bottoms which, by definition, must precede the first quarter of the market advance, is that virtually every stock is undervalued. Compared to their historical P/E ranges, most stocks are at or below the low end. Price to book value ratios yield the same conclusion. Consequently, it is easy to find undervalued stocks. In fact, finding undervalued stocks is so easy that it is difficult to make stock selections on this basis. Everything qualifies. If anything, the high-risk stocks are likely to be the most extremely undervalued, which contributes to their fine performance during the first quarter of the market advance.

THE SECOND QUARTER

The second quarter of the bull market is also a fine time to be in stocks. By now, most investors realize that the bear market has ended. While they have already missed the best part, the fun is not over. In this second quarter, growth stocks are likely to begin to assert themselves. Investors now see a good future for the economy and are looking for ways to participate in this growth. Growth stocks with smaller capitalizations than the giants often do very well. They have the most potential for inflated growth expectations. In this favorable climate, investors can often imagine tremendous growth potential in these stocks. Those smaller capitalizations mean that buying interest can move the stocks higher more quickly. At the same time, the High-Quality growth stocks are also moving ahead nicely and are probably beginning to outperform the market averages.

The risk-for-the-sake-of-risk theme may end during the second quarter, as most risk stocks have run up to something approaching fair valuation. They are no longer outstanding bargains and, from here on, must advance on their longer-term prospects. This means risk itself is no longer a plus. Some risk stocks will continue to advance on their own merits, while others will run into resistance.

This is also the quarter when undervaluation virtually disappears. For sure, some stocks will be lagging the market and will continue to appear undervalued. Others will lead the market and already be pushing into overvalued territory. It will be difficult to decide if a lagging, undervalued stock is a bargain or has just lost its earnings luster. On the other hand, stocks apparently overvalued due to their rapid rate of price advance may be overvalued or they may be the leaders of some new market theme. While these are difficult choices, the real point is that the market itself still has room to advance at this stage.

What is likely to be the theme of the second quarter? There are no good guidelines. It will probably be something related to the temperament of investors, perhaps based on their experiences during the preceding bear market. Or, it could be a new growth-related theme as some new product or service receives investor attention.

THE THIRD QUARTER

By the time the third quarter begins, the going is becoming more difficult. Many stocks have reached their peaks and begun to fade. This is true even of the Lesser-Quality growth stocks, and it may be time to think about slowly easing them out. A possible strategy during the third quarter is to slowly sell the Lesser-Quality growth stocks, switching part of the proceeds into the High-Quality growth stocks with more staying power later in the bull market, and part into cash reserves. Most of the overall market advance is now over. It is time to become very, very selective in stock picking, going for only very High-Quality growth (possibly already overvalued) and stocks that are particularly in tune because they can uniquely benefit from the coming economic difficulties. In short, preparations for the bear market should already be started.

THE FOURTH QUARTER

The fourth quarter is the most difficult of all and the time to be wrapping things up. It is time to 'winterize' the portfolio.[1] Most stocks

---

[1]This phrase is suggested by Dr. Carl Otto, a leading Montreal investment manager.

will be in downtrends and should already have been sold out of the portfolio. The High-Quality growth stocks will be on their last legs, and we should be in the process of cutting them back. How far back and how quickly is impossible to say. That is a matter of individual judgment and depends on the circumstances at the time. The only certainty is that other investors will be of little help to you. They will still be bullish and will be critical of your decision to cut back.

The theme here may be inflation or shortage stocks. The economic situation is likely to be all-out boom with the economy operating at full capacity. Shortages may turn into a market theme, providing some short-term investment or, should we say, speculative opportunities. However, a bear market is looming just ahead, so this is a risky game.

Value is also a tricky investment approach in the fourth quarter. Since most stocks will already be in downtrends, already past their peaks, they will appear to be getting back into undervalued territory. They will seem attractive, tempting investors to buy them. These stocks are already in their own bear market and will likely go much lower when the real bear market begins. Essentially, this means value can be dangerous in the fourth quarter.

Then comes the bear market. Ideally, no stocks would be held. This is too extreme for many investors, particularly institutional investors. Uncertainty is one reason. One never knows for certain what stage of the cycle we are in or that a bear market has begun. The stock market game is far too complicated. So probably the best hedge is to maintain some exposure in growth stocks, stressing high quality stocks, even if you do suspect a bear market.

In addition, there is likely to be a theme, and in a bear market the theme is often gold stocks. People become concerned over the stability of the economic system, monetary crises, and the like, and gold stocks get a play. Mainly, however, this is the time for reserves, short-term liquid assets that will probably be paying a high rate of return. Treasury bills, commercial paper, and liquid asset funds will be excellent alternatives to stocks at this time. These short-term investments will be providing high yield and safety when most stocks are dropping rapidly.

STRATEGY SUMMARY

Step One in stock market strategy is understanding your own risk tolerances. This should result in the establishment of a maximum risk exposure for your portfolio. The risk of your portfolio should then be controlled so it does not exceed this level. With a reasonably well-diversified portfolio, the market risk of individual security holdings can be averaged, weighted by their value in the portfolio, to calculate overall portfolio risk.

Step Two relates risk exposure to the outlook for the overall stock market. This is especially important since the performance of the stock market as a whole has the dominant impact on the performance of any diversified portfolio. If the market is down, the vast majority of portfolios will decline. If the market advances, most portfolios will be up.

Since evaluating the outlook for the stock market is vital, a number of guidelines have been provided. The most important is that the market anticipates economic recessions and economic recoveries. Well before a recession, even before leading economists are aware a recession is coming, the stock market will peak and start its decline. Then, six months or so before the recession ends, the stock market will bottom and start to advance. Often it bottoms and begins its advance in the face of terrible economic news. The stock market starts its upward move when pessimism reigns in economic and business circles.

Despite the stock market's remarkable economic foresight, which puts it well ahead of most forecasters, it is still possible to anticipate the major trend of the market. Techniques have been outlined for determining whether the market is in a basic uptrend or downtrend. The techniques include leading economic indicators, monetary policy and interest rates, value and technical factors. These indicators are not designed to anticipate every fluctuation in the stock market. Minor fluctuations are impossible to anticipate. When applied with judgment, the techniques will help in anticipating the major trend.

The third and final step is stock selection. Stocks should be selected with the goal of fully participating in the upward move of the stock market, not trying to find the biggest winner. Investors who concentrate their efforts on finding big winners usually have unsatisfactory investment results. Investors should attempt, up to their risk tolerances developed in Step One, to hold a diversified portfolio of solid companies in order to attain this market participation.

Three basic methods of stock selection have been outlined—value, growth, and theme stocks. Theme stocks offer the largest returns in the shortest period of time. They also offer the most risk of not participating in the market rise if you happen to guess wrong. Themes are very difficult to play, often ending just when we get invested in them.

Value is no panacea either. All things equal, an undervalued stock is preferred. However, value is not easy to determine, as most techniques rely on hindsight and historical precedent which may or may not be valid in the future. Value is even dangerous late in a bull market cycle because of the tendency for many stocks to peak before the market averages peak. An investor can be tricked into buying an apparently undervalued stock that in reality has just begun the bear market a little early. Nevertheless, value is important and should always receive consideration.

Neither is growth the whole answer. Most growth-stock advocates err greatly when they ignore the importance of market timing. It simply does not pay to hold growth stocks through bad markets. Growth stocks do combine some very attractive features. Over the long term, true growth stocks, that is, stocks whose earnings do grow, turn in favorable performances. Consequently, growth can be helpful in offsetting poor market-timing decisions and poor valuation judgments. If you buy a growth stock at too high a multiple, the earnings growth may eventually offset your error. Your investment returns may be low for a while, but you stand a good chance of eventual bailout.

Additionally, growth stocks have a fairly predictable pattern of behavior during a market cycle. They tend to start slowly, pick up speed in the second and third quarter of the bull market, and move out in front in the fourth quarter. They often hold up reasonably well far into the bear market, being among the last stocks to fall. The tendency of growth stocks to start late at the beginning of the bull market and to fall only after the bear market is well in force are very helpful characteristics. This tendency provides additional time for the investor to figure out what is happening in the stock market. Concentrating on growth stocks provides more time to decide to buy and more time to decide to sell. Since the stock market possesses so much foresight, this extra time is very important.

Finally, growth stocks have a better chance than most classes of stocks to become a new market theme. The favorable characteristics of growth stocks, the fact that so many institutional investors prefer growth stocks, and the fact that growth stocks tend to be the strongest and most dynamic companies in the economy all reinforce the probability that growth will become a new theme. It has happened frequently in the past and no doubt will again in the future.

The probable behavior of value, growth, and theme-oriented stocks along with risk-management suggestions is outlined in Exhibit 9-1.

EXHIBIT 9-1

Strategy Summary

	First Quarter	Second Quarter	Third Quarter	Fourth Quarter	Bear Market
		← Bull Market →			
Growth	May underperform market averages	Beginning to catch up with averages	Higher-quality doing well	Highest-quality strong, others declining	Likely to fall rapidly towards end of bear market
Value	All stocks undervalued	Most fairly valued, some bargains	Many stocks becoming overvalued	Advancing stocks overvalued, declining stocks deceptively undervalued	All stocks becoming undervalued
Theme	Risk-oriented	?	Possibly growth stocks	Inflation hedge, shortage stocks	Gold stocks
Risk exposure	Move toward maximum	Maximum risk exposure	Begin to reduce risk	Winterize portfolio	Minimize risk exposure

This is a summary of the recommended stock market strategy. It shows what growth stocks are likely to do at each phase, when to pay attention to value, and where to look for the market's theme. Most important, it suggests when to increase risk exposure and when to minimize risk. Short-term investments, having essentially zero risk, are the best way to minimize risk.

Note that the recommended risk exposure during the first quarter of a new bull market is "move toward maximum" and during the fourth quarter is to "winterize" the portfolio. The first and fourth quarters are key decision times when the really important investment moves are made. Decide carefully and accurately here, and you will go a long way toward improving your investment results. Moves at other times are minor compared to the decisions made here.

One conclusion of this analysis is to emphasize growth stocks as opposed to value and theme stocks during the bull market cycle. Stocks with long-term growth potential should be the dominant portion of the portfolio, though value and theme stocks should also receive consideration. Stress growth. Get value with growth when you can. Limit the resources devoted to theme stocks because of their risk.

THE REMAINING DECISIONS

Even with a stock market strategy, there are many difficult decisions to be made. We have already reviewed the question of risk. How aggressive or conservative an individual portfolio should be is a very important question and deserves very careful analysis.

Beyond this, the phase of the market cycle is also very difficult to determine. There are no hard and fast guidelines. The current economic and financial outlook must constantly be evaluated and related to the stock market. When is the next business downturn or upturn coming and how does it relate to the market cycle? Is something else more important than the business cycle at the moment? These questions must constantly be reanswered in the face of changing conditions and in competition with millions of other investors. The old random walk is always at work, you know. The apparent randomness may so confuse the situation that it is difficult to decide the current phase of the market cycle.

Stock selection remains a difficult task, even with the value, growth, and theme guidelines we have suggested. Indeed, the difficulty of stock selection, of finding those big winners before everyone else, is one of the reasons this strategy-oriented approach is recommended. The main objective should be to participate in the overall stock market advance to the extent that your risk tolerances will allow. Value, growth, and theme stocks will help you to keep up with the market. If you do a little better, fine. If you do a little worse, don't concern yourself. That concern can lead to rash, unprofitable decisions.

Value, growth, and market theme stocks also bear some relationship to the phase of the market advance. Theme stocks are particularly volatile. Stock market themes change more frequently than Paris fashions. Value, too, can be deceptive, especially late in a bull market. Apparently undervalued stocks can just as easily be those that peaked early and are already heading down. All things being equal, investors should prefer undervalued stocks to overvalued stocks. But all things are seldom equal.

Even growth stocks are tricky. Some guidelines for selecting growth stocks based on the tenets of growth-stock advocates have been recommended. The concept of sustainable growth has also been introduced. The list of growth stocks changes frequently. For one thing, the list depends on the temper of the times, and times change quickly. When Disney was at $150, it was a High-Quality growth stock. Several months later at $20, it was just another land development company. This unusually harsh example illustrates the volatility inherent in these labels.

Obviously, the application of all these concepts must be approached with due humility, respecting both the complexities involved and our own limited faculties for dealing with them. The stock market reflects the hopes and fears of millions of investors, many of whom are as smart or smarter than we are, are better informed, have more resources, and perhaps most important, have more objectivity, more stability, more cool when it counts. We must approach the market with great respect, not expecting too much and prepared to be wrong. If we cannot do this, if we lack this respect for the challenge of the competition, or worse yet, are not prepared or cannot afford to be wrong, we should not be in the market at all.

If you have the proper mental attitude and have objectively evaluated the risks, have carefully considered how much a stock or a portfolio or the market can go down—yes, even the stock or portfolio that we, in our great and egotistical wisdom have with the best advice of trained and experienced experts selected, can go down very, very substantially—then, you are prepared to begin developing the stock market strategy appropriate for you. Concentrate first on long-run investment objectives, then on the investment environment, the phase of the market cycle, and last on stock picking. Most investors do this in reverse order, and 80 percent are failures in the market. Get your priorities right, develop your stock market strategy first, and your opportunities for success will be greatly enhanced.

INDEX

INDEX